Popular Freezer Cookery

COLOUR CODING
— Meat
— Fish
— Vegetables
— Fruit
— Prepared foods

Popular
Freezer Cookery

by Mary Berry

TREASURE PRESS

A special thank you to Stephanie Blazberg and Juliet Higgens of the Home Economics Department of Philips Electrical Ltd., who lent their test kitchens for photography.

Photographs on pages 63, 71, 103 above, 107, 111, 115 by the Flour Advisory Bureau. All other photography by Jerry Tan of the Electricity Council's photographic unit.

Frontispiece:
Chest freezer. This is the most popular type of freezer if you want one with a large capacity. Colour coding is used for easy recognition of the foods.

First published by Octopus Books Limited

This edition published by Treasure Press
59 Grosvenor Street
London W1

© 1972 Octopus Books Limited

ISBN 0 907407 27 7

Printed in Hong Kong

Contents

Weights and measures 6

Is a freezer really necessary? 7

How to use your freezer 16

From fresh to frozen 28

Recipes: Getting off to a good start 50

The heart of the meal 61

A fine finish 92

Straight from the oven 110

Index 127

Weights and Measures

All measurements in this book are based on Imperial weights and measures, with American equivalents given in parenthesis.

Measurements in *weight* in the Imperial and American system are the same.
Measurements in *volume* are different, and the following table shows the equivalents:

Spoon measurements

Imperial	U.S.
1 teaspoon (5ml.)	$1\frac{1}{4}$ teaspoons
1 tablespoon (20ml.)	$1\frac{1}{4}$ tablespoons (abbrev: T)

Level spoon measurements are used in all the recipes.

Liquid measurements

1 Imperial pint	20 fluid ounces
1 American pint	16 fluid ounces
1 American cup	8 fluid ounces

Is a Freezer Really Necessary?

Why have a freezer? The early refrigerators had very small freezing compartments with room for a tray of ice cubes and little more. If you bought a packet (package) of frozen peas, you could squash it in on top of the ice cubes, and if you came home with a family block of ice cream, you dispensed with the ice and your drinks were luke-warm that evening. And that, for most people, was the full extent of their contact with home freezing.

Today, the freezer has dropped out of the luxury class. Some house-wives, particularly those who go out to work or who live in rural areas, place it high on their list of priorities. There will always be a few people who would not have a freezer if they were offered one, and some who wonder whether it really would be worth while. But the waverers nearly always come down in favour of the freezer in the end.

The reason, very simply, is that freezing is a quick and easy method of preserving food safely for several months. In the case of fruit and vege-tables, for a year until the season comes around again. This works to your advantage in two ways:
a) Food may be bought when it is cheap – a turkey, perhaps, bought when prices are at rock-bottom; soft fruits, like strawberries, picked yourself on farms at give-away prices; food sold at a discount to those who will buy it in bulk.

A freezer cuts out waste, for instance, the remainder of a cake made for a special occasion can be put into the cold store. It means, too, that a glut in the garden is food wanted not wasted. The crop may be gathered when it is young and tender. Carrots, for example, have a specially delicate flavour when pulled early; small beetroots, the size of golf balls, are very good; and young broad beans taste so different from their more mature counterparts that they could almost be another vegetable.

b) Food may be prepared and cooked when you feel like it. An empty day in your diary can be set aside for a cooking and baking spree. Such advance preparation helps with dinner parties. With each course packed away in the freezer ready to be produced and heated through on the day itself, you are released from the frenzy of work that ties you to the kitchen. No longer need you be condemned to missing the interesting bits of conversation as your guests sip their aperitifs while you are toiling in the kitchen.

There are all manner of ways to make your freezer work for you. Casseroles, for example, take about 15 minutes to prepare. Preparing three or four times the amount takes very little longer. When the casserole is cooked the surplus may be packaged in three separate containers, frozen and stored in the freezer for use later. Those few extra minutes have, in fact, given you three future meals with no preparation.

In theory, ownership of a freezer should cut the cost of living. In practice, say most freezer owners, your expenditure stays about the same, but your *standard* of living soars.

Arguments against freezers mainly occur due to fears about the quality of the food and doubts about its nutritional value. Here, perhaps, is the best place to state that as long as the temperature of the freezer is maintained at −18°C, 0°F or less, *the food will remain in the condition in which it was frozen.* Freezing slows down the process of deterioration to such an extent that it is held, so to speak, in a state of suspended animation. Slight fluctuations of temperature, the result of the door or lid of the freezer being opened, and of air circulating between the packages, may eventually cause a slight deterioration in appearance and texture. If the initial freezing took too long, this may have the same effect. Because of this, maximum storage periods are recommended for different foods and these should be followed if possible. You should remember, too, that once the food is thawed, deterioration goes on at the natural rate.

There is no magic about a freezer. It cannot improve poor quality food. The food that you put into your freezer should be in perfect condition, freshly gathered if grown in the garden, or the best you can find if bought in a market. Do not freeze vegetables which have passed their prime, nor over-ripe fruit. No freezer can turn the clock back.

Nutritionally, the freezer has no adverse effect on food. Poor cooking may cause the loss of some nutritional value, but you cannot blame this on the freezer. Freezer-stored food should taste, look and be as good as the garden-fresh product.

Getting the go-ahead

You have listened to the arguments – both for and against – and have made up your mind. You are going to buy a home freezer.

Now comes the tricky part. What type and size of freezer to buy, and at what cost. The three basic types are listed here:

a) Combined freezer/refrigerator, *see picture page* 10. The freezing compartment, which is usually on top of the refrigerator and has its own separate door, is useful mainly for storage of commercially frozen goods. Even so, it is capable of storing no more than about 50 lb. of food. The housewife can quick freeze some things herself but only small quantities at a time. A combined freezer/refrigerator would not be very practical for the rural housewife or the woman with a large family, who is planning to use her freezer for bulk storage.

b) Upright freezer, *see front cover*. This looks like a tall refrigerator and is fitted inside with shelves and wire baskets, or trays. Its main advantages are that it takes up less floor space than the chest-type of freezer, will usually fit in more conveniently to the existing arrangement of kitchen furniture, and that access to all parts of the interior is easier than with the chest freezer. On the debit side is the fact that each time the door is opened the inrush of warm air causes a slight rise in temperature, producing extra frosting on the walls and a consequent increase in running costs. Inner doors between the shelves, available on some models, will offset the loss of cold to some extent, but the saving in running costs will be adversely reflected in the purchase price. In any case, the price of an upright freezer will be more than a chest freezer of comparable capacity.

c) Chest freezer, *see frontispiece*. This is the popular choice for those seeking a freezer with a large capacity. It is usually long and narrow (so that it can be carried through a doorway without difficulty). It has a lift-up lid, which should be counterbalanced so that it will stay open in any position. The freezer takes up a large amount of floor space and requires a fair amount of space above as well to accommodate the lid when open. It is usually fitted with wire baskets or wire partitions. Since cold air is heavier than warm air, there is little temperature change when the lid is raised, and running costs are therefore very economical.

The choice of freezer to suit you and your family must be taken in the light of various factors. The following guide lines may help:

a) Size. The most common mistake to make is to choose a freezer that is *smaller* than you need. It is safer to buy the largest that you can afford and have the space for. A capacity of 12 cubic feet is probably the minimum size required by a family of four living in a rural or semi-rural position. And it is safe to bet that even then Mum will be hankering after a 16 cubic feet cabinet before her first season of ownership is out.

b) Type. This depends on where you intend to put it (see page 13) and on your own temperament. If, by nature, you are an untidy, and fairly slap-happy sort of person, a chest freezer may well be best for you, however carelessly packages are put into a chest, they won't all fall out every time you open the door! And although this may be an

Combined freezer refrigerator. Ideal when space is at a premium as both the refrigerator and freezer are in one cabinet, the freezer being at the top.

uneconomic way of running your freezer, at least you will not be trying to alter your personality with the consequent harm this can do to family harmony and stability.

You should also bear in mind your own physical size. Some chest freezers are taller than others and a small person might find it difficult, not to say hazardous, to reach the farthest corners. With an upright model you can, after all, always stand on a chair.

c) Price. For an item of this size, it pays to shop around. Many shops specialize in refrigerators and home freezers, and their prices are usually considerably lower than those recommended by the manufacturer. Most shops offer hire purchase facilities. If you are paying cash, however, many small shops will offer you a further discount. Secondhand freezers are occasionally available. The difficulty, of course, is to know whether they represent a good buy or not, but most freezers are incredibly trouble-free, giving dependable service for many years. Take care when buying a second-hand cabinet to check whether spare parts and servicing are available. Do not buy an ice cream conservator if you want a home freezer. Conservators are purely for storing frozen foods and only maintain a temperature of $-18°C$, $0°F$. This means that you cannot lower the temperature to actually freeze food.

Useful extras, found on some freezers, are listed here in order of their importance:

a) Quick freezing compartment. Frankly, I consider this essential, if the freezer is to be used to its fullest extent. It is a small compartment (up to one-tenth the capacity of the whole freezer) into which the food to be frozen can be placed so that it is separated from the frozen food already stored. The walls of the quick freezing compartment should have evaporator coils passing through them, so that the space within gets very cold very quickly.

Quick freezing compartments usually have a separate control switch and indicator light. When switched on, the effect is to by-pass the thermostatic control, so that the freezer motor continues to reduce the temperature inside the freezer. Best results in quick freezing are attained when the temperature is lowered to $-24°C$, $-12°F$ or less.

b) Internal light. However well-positioned the freezer is in relation to the lights in the room, unless you have an internal light which comes on when the lid is opened, most of the interior will be in shadow, which can make finding the package you want difficult.

c) Lock. This is particularly useful if the freezer is in a garage, especially if you and the family are out all day, and also when you go on holiday. It also prevents the children from opening and shutting the cabinet unnecessarily.

A dinner party frozen ahead. Scollops, see page 56, Osso Buco (see page 80), Strawberry Cheesecake, see page 105, rolls, see page 113 or these could be bought frozen.

Ready to serve the dinner.

Where to put it

You have bought your freezer certainly with the idea of saving yourself trouble, and possibly with the thought of saving yourself money. Obviously, the kitchen is the most accessible location for the freezer. If, however, the room is very warm or if the freezer is next to the cooker, boiler or heated drier, the freezer motor will have a great deal of work to do to keep the temperature down, and running costs will increase. It will also have to be defrosted more often. Equally, a cool, dry shed at the bottom of the garden may be low in running costs but also very inconvenient. A compromise, therefore, is preferable. A pantry, larder, back hall or lobby, even a passageway, may be ideal places for a deep freeze, provided there is sufficient space to leave a gap for air circulation between the back of the freezer and the wall. A garage may be used as long as it is near the house, but it is not an ideal situation because the garage could be damp. An open verandah is *not* suitable. If the freezer *is* to go in the garage, raise it on wood blocks to ensure that damp cannot build up underneath, but the jacking up of a chest freezer will make it that much taller and therefore more difficult to reach down inside.

One of the disadvantages of putting your freezer in a place which is visited only infrequently is that if anything goes wrong it may not be noticed in time to prevent the food inside from being ruined. If the choice of such a site is unavoidable, it is possible to fit an alarm system which will buzz or ring if the temperature in the freezer rises above a certain figure. These alarms, however, are expensive.

When things go wrong

Apart from power cuts or power failures (which you can't do anything about anyway), the most likely source of trouble is an easily accessible plug. Never let your freezer plug share a socket with any other piece of equipment. If possible, the socket should be well out of the way of 'helpful' fingers, whether children's or adults'. As an added precaution, tape both plug and switch (see picture, page 15), and stick up a notice saying 'Do not, on any account, switch off'. This is particularly important if the freezer is in the garage.

Most freezers run happily for years without giving any trouble at all. But if for any reason, the motor stops operating, there is no need to panic. Frozen food can be kept in the cabinet for up to 24 hours after an electricity failure, *provided the door or lid is kept shut.* As soon as you have made certain that the failure is not due to a blown fuse or faulty plug, telephone your maintenance engineer immediately. If the repair is going to take longer than 24 hours to carry out, most freezer firms operate an emergency service to keep your food frozen.

A sensible safeguard is insurance. Information about insuring the contents of your freezer is often included with the manufacturer's instructions when you buy the freezer.

General maintenance

External   The exterior of the freezer is usually white enamel, like a refrigerator, and looks clean and gleaming when it arrives from the shop. Enamel, however, scratches easily and can chip, which will reduce the trade-in price if you ever want to exchange your freezer. The top of the freezer soon becomes used, by most freezer-owners, for putting down shopping and all sorts of other items. It is as well, therefore, to protect the top of the freezer, as soon as it arrives, with a self-adhesive plastic.

Internal   Opening the door or lid of the freezer lets in warm air and encourages the formation of frost on the walls. The frosting should not be allowed to build up since it increases running costs and decreases efficiency. Most manufacturers recommend scraping the frost from the walls about once a month, using the scraper provided. The frosting should never reach more than $\frac{1}{4}$-inch thick. The freezer should be fully defrosted about twice a year, or according to manufacturer's instructions.

Servicing   Your freezer should be professionally serviced about once a year.

Defrosting   Speed is essential. Try to arrange to defrost when the freezer is comparatively empty and just before you restock. The night before you plan to carry out the defrosting, place plenty of newspapers in the freezer to ensure that they get really cold. Next day, remove all the frozen food, wrapping each package in layers of cold newspapers, and place it in the coldest spot available. Follow the manufacturer's instructions for raising the temperature (either by turning the temperature setting to 'defrost' or by unplugging the freezer). Bowls of boiling water placed inside the freezer will hasten the melting of the ice. In the meantime, using the scraper or a stiff brush (windscreen scrapers, sold in car accessory shops, are excellent for this purpose), remove the ice from the walls. A knife should not be used, because it can scratch the walls. When all the ice has melted, mop up the water with a cloth.

Any smells in the cabinet may be removed by wiping the inside with a solution of two teaspoons of bicarbonate of soda and one cup of vinegar to one gallon of water. Use a soft cloth to dry the inside thoroughly. Switch the freezer on again and leave it for an hour to get cold. Replace the frozen food.

Always wear gloves when you are handling frozen packages for any length of time.

A new freezer   Before using a freezer for the first time, wash it inside with warm water and dry it thoroughly. The instructions will tell you whether you should set the temperature gauge yourself or whether it has already been set before leaving the factory. Fit the appropriate plug. Remember that a freezer must only be used from an earthed socket and must never be used from a lighting point. Switch on, and leave the freezer for about 12 hours before using it.

   Tape your freezer plug up to prevent the freezer being turned off accidentally, see page 13.

How to Use Your Freezer

Proper planning is essential. Even if you are not the planning type, you owe it to that beautiful shining gorgeous monster now comfortably settled in your house to change your ways a little. The effort must be made, otherwise the whole thing is a waste of money and you might as well send the freezer back where it came from without further ado.

Proper planning means planning in *everything*. Menus should be thought out in advance so that shopping for them can be done in one session, and two or three meals can be made immediately and placed in the freezer. Certain recipes should be cooked in small quantities so that never again can unexpected visitors catch you with only a slice of dry bread in the bread bin and a piece of mouldy cheese in the refrigerator.

Your vegetable garden can be replaced – fears of a glut need worry you no longer. Bulk buying must be thought out and seasonal buying prepared for. Most important of all, you must be able to *tell at all times* just what your freezer contains.

The following list gives some idea of what the well-stocked freezer could contain. The list may be varied, of course, to suit individual needs. We, as a family, love beans, sprouting broccoli and sweet corn, and so I plan to keep a good stock of these.

From the garden: Peas, beans, carrots, beetroot, cauliflower florets, sprouting broccoli, spinach, mixed vegetables, brussels sprouts, corn on the cob, asparagus, new potatoes, strawberries, raspberries, loganberries, blackcurrants, blackberries, apple slices, peaches, apple purée and herbs.
Other fresh food: Fruit juices, fish, shellfish, meat, offal, poultry, game, double cream, cheese, unsalted butter, eggs (separated), homogenised milk.
Bakery: Pies, cakes, biscuits, breads, bread doughs, scones, Danish pastries, pizza, sandwiches, empty flan cases, prepared pastry.
Puddings: Pastries, pies, cold desserts, fruit salads, ice cream, soufflés, mousses.

Prepared dishes: Pâtés, soups, stock, sauces, stews, moussaka, lasagne, pies, casseroles, cooked meats, pancakes (both ready for filling and unstuffed), strained baby foods.

Bought frozen foods: Fish fingers, hamburgers, any of the frozen food available from the local supermarket or, in catering packs, from bulk purchase stores and frozen food suppliers.

Some foods simply do not freeze well. Due to the action of the ice crystals formed during freezing, they tend to change their state on being thawed out. These items, therefore, should not be frozen:

Green salad: discolours and goes limp and mushy.

Hard boiled eggs: go rubbery.

Eggs in their shells: the liquid expands and the shells break.

Whites and yolks of egg together: the yolks harden.

Cream with less than 40% butter fat: separates.

Cream cheese with less than 40% butter fat: separates.

Mayonnaise: separates or curdles.

Boiled potatoes and spaghetti: go mushy.

Any frozen food which has thawed out: as soon as any food begins to thaw the enzyme and bacterial action, dormant while frozen, starts up again and the food quickly spoils. However, it is quite all right to freeze a dish cooked from previously frozen ingredients.

Packing food for the freezer

Choice of container   It is most important that the food to be frozen should be packed in the container most suited to it (see packaging materials, pages 21 and 24). The freezer is at its most efficient when air circulation between and around packages is kept to the minimum, and if all packages were brick-shaped how easy this would be. The aim, therefore, should be to freeze food into blocks wherever possible.

Rigid polythene boxes make convenient containers but it would be foolish and expensive to buy masses of boxes simply for use in the freezer. Better to have just a few boxes, line them with polythene bags, fill them with whatever you intend to freeze and place them in the quick freezing compartment. Once frozen, you can remove the polythene bag with its ice-hard contents (see picture on page 43), stack the block neatly in place and use the box again. Be careful, when filling, not to spill any food between the side of the box and the bag or, when the time comes for removal, the two will have become inseparable. Care should also be taken to ensure that the bag is as wrinkle free as possible. Empty 1 lb. sugar cartons are a fairly efficient block-making substitute for rigid boxes.

Casseroles may be frozen in similar fashion. I often line casserole dishes with foil (see page 75), fill them with, say, stew and open-freeze them in the quick freezing compartment. The frozen casserole can be covered and sealed, and the dish then returned to a useful life in the kitchen. Later on,

A freezer record book saves time in the long run, see page 20.

when the casserole is to be thawed, the foil packaged may be replaced in the dish in which it was frozen.

Method not muddle

The art of packing a freezer as closely and as economically as possible is something that develops with practice. My own method has evolved by trial and error, using sometimes unconventional containers, but the important thing about it is that it works. I can say quite confidently that I know exactly what my freezer contains at any time, and, furthermore, I can find a particular item without any effort or hesitation. This is how it is done:

For a chest freezer   It is commonsense to put bulky foods that are not often needed at the bottom of the freezer underneath the baskets. It is not very practical to have to pull everything aside in an effort to find something when you *do* want it. For this reason, I pack all the bulky items in ordinary brown cardboard boxes from the grocer, and fit the boxes with string handles so that they can be lifted out easily (see *frontispiece*). The boxes rest on a layer of newspaper, which covers the floor of the freezer and serves to catch the frost that has been scraped off the wall, and also the odd pea or bean that sometimes escapes from a carelessly sealed package. I choose the boxes with care to ensure that they fit snugly into the freezer, and any that are taller than the others are cut down to the same height.

Using different colour polythene or string bags (see colour identification opposite), I pack various types of bulky foods as closely as possible into the cardboard boxes.

The baskets above are divided logically between the small packs of foods which are used more often. I keep fruit and vegetables in one basket, baked items in the second, and meat and fish in the third. I try to keep the fast-freezing compartment as free as possible, so that it is ready for use at any time, either as a temporary store for items waiting to be 'filed' in the position where they belong, or for foods in the process of freezing.

For an upright freezer   Each shelf or part-shelf should be confined to items of a particular type, using coloured bags or tags for quick identification. Grocery boxes, of course, are not needed with an upright freezer, since these freezers are usually well equipped with baskets or trays anyway. However, as with the chest freezer, it helps to keep the quick freezing compartment or shelf free and ready for freezing.

For all freezers   A chart showing exactly where the different types of food may be found could with advantage be pasted to the outside of the cabinet. Members of the family who do not go to the freezer regularly will then be able to find things without upsetting your carefully thought-out scheme. A chart would also help anyone having to take over the running of the household in an emergency.

Polythene rigid containers are good for freezing as they can be used again and again. Glass jars and yoghurt cartons are useful too.

Freezer record book   It may seem a bother to keep up, but it is well worth the extra trouble involved in keeping a proper record of everything your freezer contains. The photograph on page 18 shows how such a book is organised.

Record keeping helps in two ways. First, it ensures that cooked dishes are used in rotation and that nothing remains in the freezer longer than the recommended storage time. Second, it enables you to judge the suitable amount of any particular food to put into the freezer each year. One year, for example, I froze 25 lb. of blackcurrants, but found when the blackcurrant season came round again that I still had 10 lb. left. My record book reminded me of the amount I had started with, so I only froze half the amount of blackcurrants the second year. I now know that blackcurrants are not all that popular with my family, although I can buy them straight from the fields at a budget price.

Colour identification   I find this one of the most important aspects of freezer organisation. If only white or clear polythene packs are used, it can take ages to find what you are looking for. Instead, I follow a simple colour code, such as, Red : meat. Blue : fish. Yellow : fruit. Green : vegetables. Black : prepared dishes.

I buy large polythene bags of these five colours and into them I place several transparent bags containing the appropriate food. It is possible, but expensive, to buy lots of small coloured polythene bags, but it is cheaper to use ordinary bags, sealed with coloured twists. One large green polythene bag, for example, will contain ten or twelve smaller, ordinary bags of sprouts. Coloured labels, sold especially for use in a freezer, are a further aid to identification and are useful for sticking on to rigid boxes. You can also write straight on to the polythene bag or box, using coloured chinagraph pencils. The writing will wash off afterwards. (See picture on page 23.)

A closer look at packing materials

Polythene bags   These are the most popular form of freezer packaging. These should be of heavy-gauge polythene so that they can be moved about in the freezer without tearing. They are used for non-liquid foods.

Rigid containers   These are made either of polythene or waxed. Any food placed in the wax ones must be cool or the wax will melt. Waxed containers may be washed and used again, but washing shortens their life. It is a good idea to line the container with a polythene bag, removing it when the food is frozen. (See page 43.) The container is then being used merely as a mould and will consequently last a long time. Rigid containers are suitable for liquids, fruits, vegetables and many prepared dishes.

Aluminium foil   Like polythene, the thicker, heavy gauge is best for the same reasons. It is possible to buy foil made especially for freezing. It is used double for lids, for lining casseroles and dishes (see page 75), for

Foil containers come in all shapes and sizes. Heavy duty foil is useful for wrapping foods and lining dishes.

wrapping around sharp bones on meat and poultry, and for wrapping joints before putting them in polythene bags.

Foil dishes and plates   These are used for freezing and serving pies, pasta, and casseroles.

Foil bags   These are used for soups and casseroles. The drawback is that they are expensive and unless you are very clever and handle them extremely cautiously, they can be used only once.

Glass jars   Those with straight necks and screw tops, are ideal for grated cheese, breadcrumbs and croûtons. Most jars can withstand the cold. If you are in doubt test by filling a jar to an inch below the top with cold water and place it *inside a polythene bag* in the freezer for two days. If the jar has not cracked or broken, it is safe to use that type of jar in the future. I use instant coffee and honey jars. Whatever you put inside the the jar, always leave at least an inch of head-space above the contents to allow for expansion on freezing.

Moisture and vapour-proof paper and polythene sheeting   I rarely use these, except for wrapping meat which I then seal with freezer tape.

Freezer tape   This is an adhesive tape which will stick even under freezing conditions. Decorator's masking tape may be used. Some freezer tapes can be written on with chinagraph pencils.

Labels   These are self-adhesive and are available either plain or coloured. They are sticky under freezer conditions, and can be used on dry containers or polythene bags. Tie on labels are also available.

Twists   These are short lengths of paper-covered wire for twisting round the neck of a polythene bag to close it. They are available in white or colours.

Other equipment

Thermometer   It is useful but not essential to have a thermometer to check the freezer temperature. It should run at $-18°C$, $0°F$ or below.

Heat-sealing equipment   I find this unnecessary. Useful only if you are freezing in a big way.

Blanching equipment   The traditional heavy blanching baskets are expensive and take time to heat through. I use a chip basket for everything except peas and beans. These go into a collapsible vegetable basket (see page 27). Nylon muslin bags or white wire muslin strainers are efficient and reasonably priced (see page 26).

Saw or serrated knives   Some serrated knives and saws are sold especially for cutting frozen foods. They are expensive and I do not find them very efficient except for cutting fish, such as salmon. For the big jobs, a bushman's saw, the sort you use for cutting up logs, is best.

Buying in bulk

A bargain is only a bargain if you would have bought the item anyway at

Colour coding makes it easy to organise the foods in the freezer, i.e. use red for meat, green for vegetables, etc., see page 21.

its customary price. Much the same is true of bulk buying. What you buy in bulk *must* be food that you and your family really like. As I discovered with my blackcurrants, if you run out of storage time and have to throw away half your bulk buy, you would have done better to keep your purse firmly closed to start with.

But there *are* big savings to be made through buying in quantity. Vacuum packed bacon, for example, keeps in the freezer for two months and is well worth buying wholesale if your family eats a lot of bacon. Fish is another money-saver. Packs of fish fillets are a marvellous stand-by, often fresher than anything you can buy in a fish shop. Be wary, however, of cheap prawns. They may have been caught in warm waters and are not nearly so good as those from cold water areas. Catering packs of vegetables, weighing about 4 lb. upwards; four dozen fish fingers; gallon tubs of ice cream; all these show appreciable saving over the cost of smaller quantities. The average saving is about 33%.

Frozen food firms will deliver, usually for no extra charge provided you have ordered a minimum worth of goods. Or you can call at the depot yourself, choosing what you want from the self-service freezers. Try to get the food back to your freezer as quickly as possible, insulating it for the journey home by wrapping it in old newspapers and a thick blanket.

Bargains can usually be had in country districts. Game in mid-season is often comparatively cheap. Brussels sprouts are sometimes sold by the sack. To make your freezer pay for itself, you should try to be on the buying end when supply outstrips demand.

Blanching baskets and bags, see page 24. The larger basket is a collapsible basket. The smaller basket is a chip frying basket. The two small mesh nylon bags are the cheapest answer.

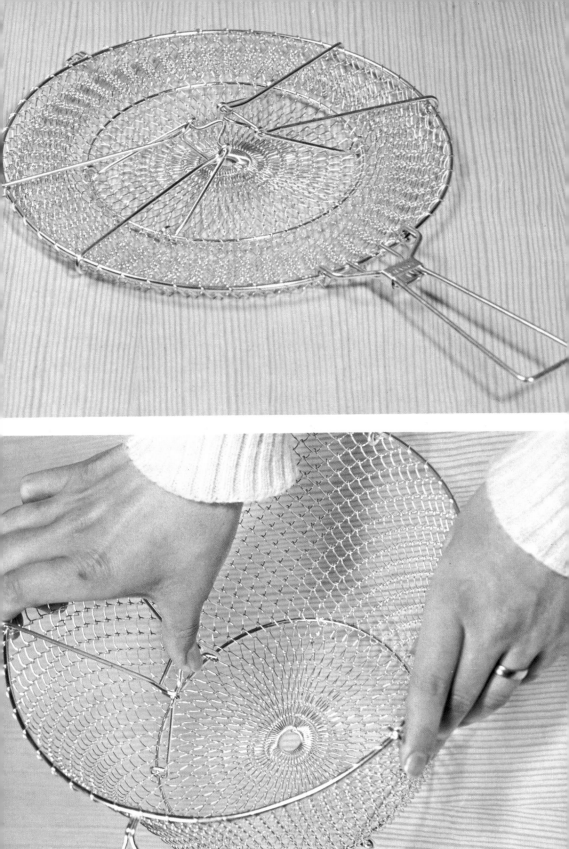

From Fresh to Frozen

General hints

1. Prepare food according to type (see freezing instructions, beginning on page 29, for meat, fish, poultry, game, vegetables, fruit, dairy produce, and prepared foods).

2. Pack so that each package contains enough for one meal for the family. Fruits and vegetables should be put in small packs, usually $\frac{1}{2}$–1 lb. in size; if larger amounts are needed, you can always use two packs. Large packs can lead to waste.

3. Pack according to type of food. Extract air from a polythene bag by sucking it out with a straw. With some foods, such as a firm chicken, it is possible just to press the air out by smoothing the bag close to the chicken towards the open end. If packing a rigid container, leave sufficient headspace to allow for expansion – about $\frac{1}{2}$ in. to 1 pint ($2\frac{1}{2}$ cups) liquid.

4. Chill in the refrigerator, if possible, before freezing. Or use iced water in the case of vegetables. The aim should be to get the food as cold as you can so that it does not warm the food already in the freezer, and freezing takes place quickly.

5. Seal packages. Attach label giving contents, date and number of servings or weight.

6. Freeze quickly. See freezer manufacturer's instruction book.

7. Thawing before use depends on the food. Prepared dishes and meat may be thawed overnight in the refrigerator before being cooked or re-heated. Vegetables are usually placed, still frozen, in boiling water. Fruit should be thawed slowly and either served as it is or used for pies and puddings.

Fuller instructions on freezing and freezing charts are given in the separate, specialised sections that follow.

Folded collapsible blanching basket.

Open collapsible blanching basket.

Fish
Fish for freezing *must* be fresh. Do not attempt to freeze it unless you have
caught it yourself, or know for certain when it was caught. Clean well
and pack each fish individually. For very small fish, such as sprats and
whitebait, freeze in $\frac{1}{2}$ lb. units in square or oblong polythene containers,
having covered with cold water first. Freeze until firm then remove from
container and put in polythene bags. Storage time: cooked fish and
shellfish, 3 months; all other fish, 6 months. Thaw overnight in the
refrigerator.

Vegetables   See chart, page 37.

Fruit   See chart, page 42.

Dairy produce
Butter   Buy when cheap. Wrap blocks in foil. Storage time: salted,
6 months; unsalted, 12 months.
Cheese   Hard cheeses keep best when grated. Ungrated, they may become
crumbly. Cream cheese with over 40% butter fat content may be frozen.
Rich, cheese dips freeze well. Storage time: hard cheese, 6 months; all
other cheese, 3 months. Thaw in refrigerator overnight, then allow one
day at room temperature for the full flavour to return.
Cream   Double cream or thick cream (i.e. with over 40% butter fat)
freezes well. Pipe cream rosettes on to foil and open freeze (see page 47).
Pack in polythene containers and use to decorate puddings and cakes.
Storage time: 3 months.
Eggs   Only freeze fresh eggs. Freezing hardens egg yolks, so the yolks
must be broken up beforehand. Yolks and whites may be mixed together
in a bowl (but not beaten) before freezing. Alternatively, freeze yolks
and whites separately. Whites may be frozen just as they are; yolks
should be mixed with salt or sugar before freezing (use 2 teaspoons of the
appropriate stabiliser for savoury or sweet uses to 1 pint ($2\frac{1}{2}$ cups) of
egg yolks). For ease of storage, open freeze in ice-cube trays and when
frozen store cubes in polythene bags. When thawed, the whites are
useful for making meringues. Storage time: 6 months. Thaw at room
temperature for 40 minutes.
Margarine, lard and cooking fat   Storage time: 5 months.
Milk   Only freeze homogenised milk. Keep it in its cartons. Storage
time: 1 month.
Baby foods   With three children under four, I know what joy it is to have
a freezer. Whenever I have time, I purée the baby's food, pack it in old
yogurt cartons and freeze it. It represents a great saving in cost compared
with canned baby food.
   I found it particularly useful when I had just one toddler for whom to

prepare a meal. A yogurt carton contains just enough for one small child and I used to keep a ready supply of minced beef, creamed fish or liver in gravy. With more than one child to cook for, it is possible to pack sufficient for them in foil dishes. I usually try to make enough at one time for all the children's meals for two weeks. When cooking for grown-ups, I find that the dish usually yields sufficient to set aside some for the children.

Useful standbys

Ice cubes   The most important in my opinion, maybe because I am always being asked for more for drinks. I keep plenty in polythene bags which is so much easier than having to empty ice cube trays at a busy moment.

Flavoured ice cubes   Stock: reduce by boiling to make a concentrated stock, season well and freeze in ice tray. Orange juice: freeze cubes of concentrated orange, and use for drinks and flavouring, (see picture, page 35). Mint cubes and herb cubes: (see page 40). Store cubes in polythene bags.

Whole Seville oranges   Buy when in season, freeze in polythene bags and use later for making marmalade. The method that uses the whole fruit is best for frozen oranges.

Croûtons   Fry bread, drain, cool and pack in glass jars. Take out croûtons as required for soup.

Grated cheese   Pack grated mature cheese as for croûtons. I once bought a quantity of grated Parmesan cheese home from a holiday in Italy and it lasted for months.

Breadcrumbs   Freeze fresh white breadcrumbs, after weighing, packing and labelling. Use for sauce and stuffings.

Sandwiches   Make sandwiches from very fresh bread, buttering well and removing crusts. Avoid fillings which do not freeze well (see page 17). Wrap in foil and seal or pack in polythene bags. Label. Storage time: 6 months.

Eggs   Pack whites and yolks separately (see page 29).

Chicken carcasses for stock   Pack in polythene bags, freeze and store in freezer until you have two or three carcasses. Then use to make chicken broth which can itself be frozen into concentrated stock cubes.

Scones   After cooking, cool, pack in polythene bag and seal. Scones can, if necessary, be taken straight from the freezer and thawed in the oven (see page 120).

Sausage rolls   Make large quantity, using home-made short-crust pastry or bought puff pastry. Cook, cool, and seal in polythene bag. Use as required.

Hot-cross buns   Freeze as soon as they have cooled after baking. Thaw out number required, re-heat in oven.

Prepared onions   Chop or slice. Freeze in $\frac{1}{4}$ lb. packs. Use as required.

Freeze small quantities of baby food, such as apple purée, each enough for one meal, see page 29.

Diced vegetables   Pack in $\frac{1}{4}$ lb. packs ready to add to soups and casseroles.
Apples   Windfall apples which normally would not keep very long can be peeled, cored and sliced, weighed into 1 lb. packs and frozen. Use when cooking apples are expensive.
Milk   Store homogenised milk in the freezer.
Bread   Sliced bread for toasting can be put in the toaster still frozen, and toasted for a little longer than usual.
Fish fingers/beefburgers/chipped potatoes and other vegetables in catering packs   These are of the greatest value to anyone with a young family.
Ice cream in gallon tubs, home-made ice lollies   Bought ice cream is the easiest pudding and when bought in bulk it is often cheaper than custard.

An answer to any question
How does freezing actually preserve food?
Freezing causes the bacteria, which would normally make fresh food decay, to lie dormant, provided that the food is kept at a temperature of −18°C, 0°F or less.

What is freezer burn?
Meat, fish or poultry which have not been properly wrapped and sealed may get greyish-white marks on their surface. These marks, known as freezer burn, may also be found on frozen food which has been stored too long. The marks are caused by dehydration and their effect is to make the surface of the food become very dry and tough.

Can frozen food be re-frozen once it has been thawed?
Fresh food freshly thawed may be refrozen quite safely since deterioration is likely to be slight. But you should know just how fresh it was when it was frozen originally. Generally speaking, it is safer to cook frozen food before re-freezing.

Is there a limit to the amount of food I can freeze at one time?
Yes. The exact amount depends on the size of the freezer, so consult the manufacturer's instructions for the figure in your case. The danger of freezing too much at once is that the food will not freeze quickly enough and it may raise the temperature of the food already stored above the safe limit.

I notice that a deposit appears to have formed on some of my frozen fruit. It looks greyish, not unlike mould. Is it dangerous?
No. It is simply sucrose hydrate which is harmless and appears sometimes when sugar is packed with fruit. It disappears on thawing.

What is headspace?
This is space left at the top of containers when liquid or semi-solid food is poured in. This space must be left, as it leaves room for the food or liquid to expand during freezing without the lid being pushed off the container.

Must I blanch vegetables before freezing?
If you want good results, yes. There is, in fact, no danger to health if you don't want to blanch, but the vegetables will not keep in the freezer for more than a month. They will also appear pale in colour.

What happens if I let frozen food over-run the recommended storage times? Is *this* dangerous?
No. There is no risk of food poisoning. However, fat foods may tend to taste a bit rancid. Other foods, in time, will develop off flavours. Most prepared cooked dishes are best used within 3 months of freezing.

What is *deep* freezing?
This is essentially a *commercial* process which cools food by blasts of very cold air (−73°C or −100°F).

Freezing Meat
There are two essentials when freezing meat: first, only freeze meat that has been hung for the correct length of time. Your butcher should do this for you and, if he has a large freezer, may even freeze the meat ready for you to transfer it to your own freezer. Second, if freezing your own meat, quick freeze only small quantities at a time.

Resist the temptation to buy more than your family can eat within the prescribed storage time, and confine your order to cuts that you know your family enjoys. Choose joints of the right size. Bear in mind that joints will keep longer in the freezer than chops and cutlets because the surface area of joints in relation to their size is less than with small cuts of meat.

Take the trouble to discuss your needs with your butcher or supplier, and do not make the mistake I made. I bought half a pig, thinking, but not checking, that the skin would be scored (we love crackling). The butcher froze it for me and I never discovered that the skin was not scored until I got the joints home. I now know that what looks a simple task when you see the butcher scoring joints of pork in the shop is in fact extremely difficult!

If the joints are very large, it is worth while getting your butcher to bone them – or bone them yourself – but again the butcher will do this far quicker than either you or I could do it. Boned meat takes up less room in the freezer.

Preparation

Meat joints　Any excess fat or gristle should be trimmed before wrapping the joint in cotton stockinette for protection. Place the meat in a polythene bag, weigh, seal, label and freeze. Meat which is to be stored for only a short while may be wrapped in freezer paper or foil, sealed round the joins with tape. Storage time: beef, 12 months; lamb, 12 months; pork, 8 months.

Steaks, chops and cutlets　Trim, wrap in fours, sixes or eights (see picture on page 39) or open freeze (see page 47). Pack in polythene bags, seal, label and freeze. Storage times: beef, 6 months; lamb, 6 months; pork, 3 months.

Offal　Trim off excess fat, wash well and dry. Weigh and pack in polythene bags. Seal, label and freeze. Storage time: 4 months.

Minced meat　Use lean meat. Weigh and measure into polythene bags. Seal, label and freeze. Storage time: 4 months.

Bacon and sausages　Measure into 1 lb. portions and wrap well. Storage time: sausages, unsmoked bacon, 3 months; vacuum-packed bacon, 2 months; smoked bacon, 1 month; bacon joints, 3 months.

Dog meat　A useful budget buy. Your butcher or supplier will quote you a special price for dog meat. Measure into appropriately sized portions, place in polythene bags. Seal, label (very clearly!) and freeze.

Poultry and game　Before freezing chickens, they should be hung for about three to four days. This means taking a freshly plucked and cleaned bird (do not wash it out) and keeping it on a china or marble slab in a cool larder for the allotted period. A well hung bird has excellent flavour. After hanging, pack giblets separately and freeze bird unstuffed. Wash the inside of the bird after thawing.

Follow the same procedure for game birds, except that they should be hung by the neck before plucking. Larger game birds, like pheasant, need to be hung for just over a week.

Label chickens 'boiling' or 'roasting' and game 'young' or 'old' for roasting or casseroling. Storage time: chicken and game, 12 months; turkey, goose, duck, 8 months.

Thawing and cooking

I prefer to thaw raw meat overnight in the refrigerator. It stays in its original wrapping, thaws slowly and there is little or no blood drip from the meat. However, I know how easy it is to forget to take the meat out of the freezer the night before, and the chart on page 36 shows how much time can be saved by thawing the meat at room temperature. If you must, it is possible and quite safe to cook meat from the frozen state, but I do not think it gives very satisfactory results, particularly with large pieces, and, since it has to stay longer in the oven, you use more fuel. I do not recommend cooking pork from frozen, and it may be dangerous to thaw it at room temperature. Pork, in fact, must always be thawed in the

Ice cube trays can be used to make fresh orange juice cubes for drinks or for flavouring and for freezing herbs and mint. Charts on page 40.

refrigerator. If you forget to put it in the refrigerator the night before, it is better to change your menu and have lamb instead! And do not be tempted to have chicken instead – that, too, should be fully thawed before cooking.

Roasting

Thaw first if possible. It is unsatisfactory to roast boned beef or lamb from from the frozen state. Beef or lamb on the bone, however, may be roasted from the frozen state, since bone is a good conductor. When cooking from the frozen state at 350°F Mark 4, allow the following times:

Joints under 4 lb. –   beef, 30 minutes to the lb. and 30 minutes over.
                          lamb, 35 minutes to the lb. and 35 minutes over.
Joints 4 lb. upwards – beef, 35 minutes to the lb. and 35 minutes over.
                          lamb, 40 minutes to the lb. and 40 minutes over.

Pot-roasting

Joints may be cooked from frozen state. Seal cut surface with hot fat to prevent the juices from being lost.

Boiling

Boiling from frozen is not recommended, as it leads to loss of weight and flavour.

Stewing

Safe to cook from frozen state, providing the meat is already cut up. Trying to dice frozen meat without thawing it is a Herculean task, guaranteed to cost you dearly in both time and temper.

Grilling (broiling) and frying

If you like it this way, all grilling (broiling) and frying may be done from the frozen state.

Thawing times

Meat	Time to allow for thawing	
	In the refrigerator	At room temperature
Joints		
Beef and lamb	5 hours a lb.	2 hours a lb.
Pork	5 hours a lb.	NOT at room temperature
Steaks and chops	6 hours a lb. ($\frac{1}{2}$ in, thick)	1–2 hours a lb.
	8 hours a lb. (1 in. thick)	2–3 hours a lb.
Chickens	12–16 hours (under 4 lb.)	NOT at room temperature
	1–1$\frac{1}{2}$ days (4 lb. and over)	NOT at room temperature
Turkeys	1–2 days (under 18 lb.)	NOT at room temperature
	2–3 days (18 lb. and over)	NOT at room temperature
Chicken portions	5–6 hours per lb.	NOT at room temperature

Freezing vegetables

Choose young small vegetables that are really fresh for the very finest results. New potatoes the size of a large marble, delicious for a special lunch, baby carrots and runner beans picked when there is hardly a sign of a bean inside.

I have included herbs, mint and parsley in vegetables, as they just don't seem to fit in anywhere else!

It is easy to freeze vegetables. There are just a few essential points for success (see step-by-step pictures of freezing brussels sprouts, page 43).

Blanching This is plunging in boiling water for a given length of time. This preserves the colour and flavour. Blanching times in the charts are taken *after* food has been added to the boiling water, and a full rolling boil has been reached.

Cooling This must be done rapidly in running water or in iced water until the vegetable is cold right through.

Draining Drain first in blanching basket or colander, then on kitchen paper, or a tea towel on newspaper.

Packing and Labelling Pack in a suitable container according to type of vegetable. Pack in one-meal sized packs. I do most of mine in half pounds, then you are sure not to waste any.

Vegetable	Special Tips	Preparation Method and Packing for the Freezer	Thawing and Cooking
Artichokes (Globe)	Choose large chokes	Cut off stalk and remove outer leaves. Blanch a few at a time in plenty of boiling water. Tightly pack each in a polythene bag. Blanching time: 6 minutes (small), 8 minutes (large). Storage time: 12 months.	Plunge frozen in boiling, salted water for about 5 minutes until outer leaves can be removed easily.
Asparagus	Buy when in season and cheapest. Stalks can also be frozen and used for soup.	Grade according to thickness of stem. Cut in to even lengths. Scrape lower part of stem. Tie in $\frac{1}{4}$ lb. or convenient-sized bundles. Blanching time: 4 minutes (thick spears), 2 minutes (thin spears). Storage time: 12 months.	Plunge frozen in boiling, salted water for 3–5 minutes.
Aubergines Eggplants	Choose ripe and medium-sized.	Peel and cut in $\frac{3}{4}$ in. slices. Blanch and open-freeze, see page 47. Pack in polythene containers. Blanching time: 3 minutes. Storage time: 12 months.	Plunge frozen in boiling, salted water for 5 minutes, or thaw and use for Moussaka —see page 87.
Beans (Broad)	Pick when young and at their best.	Pod grade in sizes, discarding any starchy ones. Pack in polythene bags or polythene containers. Blanching time: 2 minutes (small), 3 minutes (medium). Storage time: 12 months.	Plunge frozen in boiling, salted water for 5–8 minutes.

Vegetable	Special Tips	Preparation Method and Packing for the Freezer	Thawing and Cooking
Beans (French)	Will stay stiff and fresh for 24 hours after picking if wrapped in plenty of newspaper and kept in a cool place or in a refrigerator.	Top and tail. Grade, cutting the larger ones in $1\frac{1}{2}$ in. pieces. Pack in polythene bags or polythene containers. Blanching time: 2 minutes (cut beans), 3 minutes (whole beans). Storage time: 12 months.	Plunge frozen in boiling, salted water about 5 minutes for cut beans or 7 minutes for whole beans.
Beans (Runner)	Finely sliced beans do not freeze well. They lose their crispness. See above for keeping stiff for slicing.	String, top and tail. Slice into even $\frac{1}{4}$ in. diagonal slices. Blanching time: 2 minutes. Storage time: 12 months.	Plunge frozen in boiling, salted water for 5–8 minutes.
Beetroot	Pick when about the size of a golf ball – no bigger.	Cook in boiling, salted water until just tender. Peel. Pack in polythene bags. N.B. If slightly larger beetroots are used, slice before packing. Storage time: 6–8 months.	Thaw in refrigerator 2–6 hours according to size of pack.
Broccoli	Choose compact heads with tender stalks.	Remove outer leaves and trim off woody stems. Pack in polythene containers. Blanching time: 2 minutes (thick stems), 1 minute (thin stems). Storage time: 12 months.	Plunge frozen in boiling, salted water for 5–8 minutes.
Brussels Sprouts	If buying in bulk, choose button ones.	Trim and grade – no need to put crosses on the bottom. Pack in polythene bags or polythene containers. Blanching time: $1\frac{1}{2}$ minutes (small), 3 minutes (medium). Storage time: 12 months.	Plunge frozen in boiling, salted water for 5–8 minutes.
Carrots	Really tiny, whole carrots freeze well.	Grade according to size. Scrub small and scrape large carrots. Slice or dice large carrots. Pack in small amounts in polythene bags or polythene containers. Blanching time: 3 minutes (small), 4 minutes (thick slices). Storage time: 12 months.	Plunge frozen in boiling, salted water. Cook for about 5 minutes. Diced or sliced can also be added frozen to stews and casseroles.
Cauliflower	Choose only compact white cauliflowers.	Break into florets about $1\frac{1}{2}$–2 in. across. Pack in polythene bags or polythene containers. Blanching time: 3 minutes. Storage time: 12 months.	Plunge frozen in boiling, salted water for 5–8 minutes.
Celery	Use young heads. Only suitable for serving cooked.	Trim off any green. Cut in $\frac{1}{2}$ in. slices. Pack in small quantities in polythene bags. Blanching time: 3 minutes. Storage time: 12 months.	Add to stews and casseroles.

Freezing chops, cutlets or steaks
Method 1. Place a piece of polythene wrapping or druggists wrap or foil between each chop to keep them from sticking together. Wrap in polythene sheeting or druggists wrap, seal with freezer tape (special tape that withstands low temperatures). Label and freeze.
Method 2. Open freeze chops until frozen, about 8 hours.
Then pack in polythene bags, seal and label. This is the quickest way of freezing chops and freezing them separately first means that they don't stick together.

Vegetable	Special Tips	Preparation Method and Packing for the Freezer	Thawing and Cooking
Chicory	Only suitable for serving cooked.	Select only fresh white heads. Remove any discoloured leaves. To keep white add juice of ½ lemon to blanching water. Drain well after blanching. Pack in polythene bags or polythene containers. Blanching time: 3 minutes. Storage time: 12 months.	Plunge frozen in boiling salted water, with 1 teaspoon sugar added, for 8 minutes. Serve with white or brown sauce.
Corn-on-the-Cob	Essential that it is young and fresh	Remove husk and silk. Cut off stem. Pack in polythene bags, singly. It is not so satisfactory if corn kernels are taken off the cob. If preparing this way, scrape off after blanching. Blanching time: 4–6 minutes. Storage time: 12 months.	Thaw before cooking, otherwise the inside of the cob will still be cold when the corn is cooked. When thawed boil in salted water for about 5 minutes.
Courgettes	Pick young, even-sized courgettes.	Cut in half if small or in 1 in. slices of larger. Pack in polythene bags. Blanching time: 1 minute. Storage time: 12 months.	Plunge frozen in boiling, salted water for about 3 minutes, then toss in butter, or allow to thaw and sauté in butter.
Fennel	Only suitable for serving cooked.	Prepare as celery. Blanching time: 3 minutes. Storage time: 12 months.	Add to stews or casseroles (very little goes a long way) or plunge frozen in boiling, salted water for about 8 minutes and serve with cream sauce.
Herbs	Sprigs of herbs keep their colour but go limp on thawing, but are useful for flavour and for bouquet garni. (For mint, see below).	Chop herbs – separately or mixed. Either pack in clean 1 oz. ex-butter containers (the kind you get on planes) or in ice trays and cover with water. Freeze, then turn out cubes and pack in polythene bags. Storage time: 12 months.	Add to stews, casseroles, soups or sauces. The chopped herbs can be used for dips, flavouring, cheeses, etc.
Kohl Rabi	Choose small young roots.	Trim and peel. Leave very small ones whole and cube larger ones. Pack in polythene bags. Blanching time: 3 minutes (whole), 1 minute (cubed). Storage time: 12 months.	Plunge frozen in boiling, salted water for 8–12 minutes.
Marrow		Prepare as courgettes [zucchini] only in bigger pieces, removing skin if tough. Blanching time: 2 minutes. Storage time: 12 months.	Plunge frozen in boiling, salted water for about 5 minutes.
Mint Sauce	Freeze in cubes, Pick all the mint early in the season when full of flavour.	Chop finely, Divide among ice cube tray sections. Pour over sugar syrup made with 8 oz. [1 cup] sugar and ½ pint [1 cup] water. Freeze, then put cubes in polythene bag. Storage time: 12 months.	To use place one or two cubes in sauceboat. Thaw a little, then thin down with vinegar.

Mushrooms	Freeze only fresh cultivated mushrooms. Small ones are best.	Wipe clean and slice if larger than button. Sauté in butter or freeze raw. Pack in small polythene containers. Storage time: 3 months (cooked), 1 month (raw).	Add frozen cooked mushrooms to soup, sauces, casseroles or other dishes. Thaw raw mushrooms in container in refrigerator.
Onion	Take care to label onions whether mild or strong. Not suitable for salads.	Peel and cut in $\frac{1}{2}$ in. slices. Pack in polythene bags. Put in second bag if storing for some time to prevent transfer of flavour. Blanching time: 2 minutes. Storage time: 6 months.	Add to soups, stews and casseroles.
Parsnips	Choose young roots.	Prepare as Kohl Rabi. Blanching time: 4 minutes (small), 2 minutes (cubed). Storage time: 12 months.	Plunge frozen in boiling, salted water for about 15 minutes whole, 10 minutes cubed.
Peas	Use only young peas.	Pod and pack in polythene bags or polythene containers. Blanching time: 1 minute. Storage time: 12 months.	Plunge frozen in boiling, salt water for 4–7 minutes.
Peas (Mange Tout or Sugar Peas or Podded peas)	Choose flat, tender young pods.	Top and tail. Remove any strings. Blanch in small quantities. Pack in polythene bags or polythene containers. Blanching time: 1 minute. Storage time: 12 months.	Plunge frozen in boiling, salted water for about 5 minutes.
Peppers – red or green	Freeze colours separately.	Freeze whole without blanching, or halve, cut out stem and seeds and blanch. Pack whole peppers in polythene bags and cut peppers in polythene bags or polythene containers. Blanching time: 3 minutes. Storage time: 6 months (raw), 12 months (blanched).	Use raw peppers for grills. Use halved peppers for stuffing or add to dishes. Plunge frozen in boiling, salted water for 5–10 minutes according to use.
Potatoes (new)	Freeze only small ones.	Scrape or scrub. Grade into very small and small. Pack in polythene bags, with a sprig of mint in each. Blanching time: 5 minutes small, 4 minutes very small. Storage time: 6 months.	Plunge frozen in boiling, salted water for about 10 minutes.
Potatoes (new) (cooked)	If preferred they may be cooked before freezing. Slightly undercook in usual way with mint. Toss in butter.	Pack in polythene bags or polythene container. Storage time: 3 months (cooked)	Thaw. Reheat in the melted butter.
Potatoes (old) (duchesse)	These are best not browned before freezing.	Make in usual way and pipe on to trays, then open-freeze Pack in polythene containers. Storage time: 3 months.	Thaw, glaze and brown at 400°F, Mark 6 about 15 minutes.
(Croquettes)	These freeze well. If liked grated cheese can be added.	Make in usual way, toss in browned breadcrumbs. Open-freeze (page 47). Pack in polythene containers. Storage time: 3 months.	Thaw, fry in deep fat until browned, about 4 minutes.

(chipped)	Home-made fried potato crisps freeze well, too.	Blanch crisps in fat or oil at 385°F, drain well, then open freeze (page 47). Pack in polythene bags. Storage time: 3 months.	Thaw, fry in small batches in deep fat at 395°F, until brown.
Spinach	Only use youg tender spinach.	Wash well in several waters. Blanch in small quantities. Drain thoroughly, press out excess moisture. Pack in polythene bags or polythene containers. Blanching time: 2 minutes. Storage time: 12 months.	Plunge frozen in pan with $\frac{1}{2}$ in. water and little salt. Cover, cook for 5 minutes, stirring frequently. Drain well. Add butter.
Tomatoes (whole)	Whole tomatoes freeze but are not suitable for salads.	Skin tomatoes by dipping in boiling water, then slipping off the skins. Grade and pack in fours and sixes in polythene containers. Storage time: 12 months.	Thaw, preferably in refrigerator, or add to stews, casseroles etc.
Tomatoes (pulp/purée)	This is easy if you have a blender.	Skin tomatoes. Slowly simmer in own juice until tender, reduce to purée. Pack in small polythene containers or freeze in ice cube tray as herb cubes. Storage time: 12 months.	Add to soups, stews or casseroles.
Turnips	Choose young roots.	Prepare as parsnips. Blanching time: 4 minutes (small), 2 minutes (cubed) Storage time: 12 months.	Plunge frozen in boiling, salted water for about 15 minutes whole, 10 minutes cubed.

Freezing fruit

Freezing is the quickest and certainly the easiest way of preserving fruit. Most fruits do not even need blanching.

In the charts I have in some cases given a choice of the actual method of freezing certain fruits. This will depend on what you are going to do with the fruit on thawing – make jam, use for fruit salad, or for a purée for, say, apple sauce, or use in puddings or pies. See pictures on pages 46, 47.

Syrup strengths It is very much a matter of personal taste how sweet you like your fruit. I have suggested two strengths – a heavy 45% syrup and a medium 30% syrup. Always add cold syrup to the fruit and make enough to cover the fruit. Half a pint ($1\frac{1}{4}$ cups) is enough to cover about one pound of fruit (see step-by-step picture on page 47).

For 45% heavy syrup use 1 lb. (2 cups) sugar to 1 ($2\frac{1}{2}$ cups) pint water.

For 30% medium syrup use $\frac{1}{2}$ lb. (1 cup) sugar to 1 ($2\frac{1}{2}$ cups) pint water.

Blanching vegetables
Plunge prepared vegetable into fast boiling water, bring to the boil again and boil for required time.
Cool vegetables quickly in iced or running water.
Drain on kitchen paper or teacloth on newspaper.
Line polythene container with polythene bag and fill with required amount of vegetable.
Seal with a tie twist and freeze for 8 hours until frozen.
Remove bag from polythene container. The bag will have taken the shape of the container which is practical for stacking in the freezer. Label. The container is free for further freezing.

Ascorbic acid (vitamin C)   This is added to the cold sugar syrup before pouring over the fruit to help to retain the colour in fruits such as peaches and pears. To each pint (2½ cups) of syrup, add ¼ teaspoon of ascorbic acid (about 400 mg.); buy it at chemists. The powder is cheaper than the tablets.
Layering fruit with sugar   (See step-by-step picture on page 47.) Use castor (superfine) sugar. On thawing, the sugar will make its own syrup when combining with the juice which comes out from the fruit. This is ideal for fruits to be served in fruit salad or for pies and flans.
Packing   Pack fruits in suitable packs. Obviously syrup needs a polythene container and the same goes for fruits layered with sugar, as juice comes out on thawing. Leave headspace in container packs (see page 33). Seal and label.
Thawing fruits   When the fruit is to be served raw, thaw slowly in its container, preferably in the refrigerator. Most fruits are best very cold and slightly frozen. It takes about 6 hours to thaw a one pound pack in the refrigerator.

If the fruit is to be cooked, thaw fruit at room temperature until the individual fruits are separate, then cook gently so as not to break up the fruit.

Fruit	Special Tips	Preparation Method and Packing for the Freezer	Use
Apples	Method 1 is for good quality cookers, i.e. Bramleys. Label purée according to sugar content. Method 2 and 3 take up less room in freezer.	Peel, core and slice. To prevent browning during preparation stand in salt water. 1. Blanch 1 minute, drain thoroughly. Pack in polythene bags or polythene containers or 2. Stew with sugar–4 oz. [½ cup] to 1 lb. apples, and pack as above or 3. Stew until tender with or without sugar. Reduce to a purée and pack as above. Storage time: 12 months.	1. For blending with other fruit, pie fillings or crumbles. 2. For strudels, pies or apple puddings. 3. For apple sauce or baby foods.
Avocado Pears	Only freeze purée. It loses texture if frozen whole.	Remove stone. Scoop out flesh, mash with lemon juice – 1 tablespoon [1¼ T] to each avocado. Pack in small polythene containers. Storage time: 3 months.	For avocado dip, sandwich filling or soup.
Blackberries	Choose firm, ripe fruit. Pick on a dry day.	Wash if necessary, drain thoroughly. Pack in small quantities in polythene containers. Storage time: 12 months.	Any kind of pudding or sauce.

44

Cherries	Choose sweet, ripe cherries. Red freeze better than black. White cherries are best covered with syrup.	Remove stalks. Wash if necessary. Stone if liked. 1. Pack in polythene bags, do not stone. or	1. For pies and flans.
		2. Layer in dry sugar—4 oz. [½ cup] sugar to 1 lb. stoned cherries. Pack in polythene containers. or	2. For pies, puddings and flans.
		3. Cover with 45% syrup (see page 42). Pack as above. Storage time: 12 months.	3. For ice cream topping—add a little kirsch after cooking and cooling.
Currants (black, red and white)	Choose ripe, firm fruit. Blackcurrants have the finest flavour, so are best for method 4.	Remove stems. Wash if necessary. Dry thoroughly. 1. Pack in polythene containers or	1. For jam making.
		2. Layer in dry sugar—6 oz. [¾ cup] sugar to 1 lb. fruit. Pack as above. or	2. For pies, puddings and crumbles.
		3. Cover fruit with 45% sugar syrup (see page 42). Pack as above. or	3. Serve as stewed currants.
		4. Blackcurrant purée. Stew with sugar—6 oz. [¾ cup] to 1 lb. fruit. Reduce to a purée. Pack in small polythene containers. Storage time: 12 months.	4. For flavouring ice cream or for fruit drinks.
Gooseberries	Method 1 is easy but takes up more freezer space. Use slightly under-ripe fruit for jam-making, for pies, crumbles and stewing.	Top and tail. Wash if necessary. 1. Pack in polythene bags or	1. For jam-making, pies, crumbles and stewing.
		2. Stew with 4–6 oz. [½ – ¾ cup] sugar to 1 lb. fruit. Reduce to purée. Pack in small polythene containers. Storage time: 12 months.	2. For fools and flavouring ice cream.
Greengages	Choose ripe fruit without blemishes. Covering with syrup is not recommended as the skins toughen on storage.	Wash if necessary. Dry. Cut in half and remove stones. Pack in polythene containers. Cover with 45% syrup (see page 42). Storage time: 12 months.	For pies, crumbles and puddings.
Loganberries	Choose firm, ripe fruit. Pick on a dry day.	Wash if necessary, drain thoroughly. Pack in small quantities in polythene containers. Storage time: 12 months.	For puddings and sauces.
Nectarines	See peaches below.		
Oranges (sweet)	Buy when cheap.	Peel, remove pith and pips and slice. Layer in sugar—6 oz. [¾ cup] to about 4 oranges. Storage time: 12 months.	Use for adding to fruit salad or serving alone. Add liquor, if liked, after thawing.

Freezing fruit. Some fruits such as rhubarb, gooseberries, raspberries, red, white and blackcurrant may be frozen simply by packing into polythene bags or polythene containers.

2.

4.

Fruit	Special Tips	Preparation Method and Packing for the Freezer	Use
Oranges (bitter)	Buy in season.	Pack in polythene bags. Label, giving weight of oranges. Storage time: 12 months.	Use for marmalade making. The whole fruit method is best. Simmer whole fruit until tender, then cut up with knife and fork. Remove pips. Boil up with the water in which the fruit was cooked for 10 minutes. Strain. Return fruit to pan with strained liquid. Boil off excess water, if necessary, and proceed as usual.
Peaches	Peaches freeze well. Use ascorbic acid to prevent discolouration (see page 44).	Blanch 1 minute. Lift off skin and cut in half if liked. At once poach in 30% syrup (see page 42) for 2 minutes. Drain and cool. Add $\frac{1}{4}$ teaspoon ascorbic acid to 1 pint [2$\frac{1}{2}$ cups] cold syrup. Pour over fruit. As fruit tends to float, cover first with a piece of crumpled waxed paper or greasproof paper before packing in polythene containers. Storage time: 12 months.	For serving ice cold as a dessert. For special occasions add brandy – about 1 tablespoon [1$\frac{1}{4}$T] for 4 peaches, after thawing.
Pears	Pears have a delicate flavour and do not freeze as well as other fruits. Choose unblemished, slightly under-ripe fruit. Use ascorbic acid to prevent discolouration (see page 44).	Wash if necessary, peel and core. At once poach in 30% syrup (see page 42) for 2 minutes. Drain and cool. Add $\frac{1}{4}$ teaspoon ascorbic acid to 1 pint [2$\frac{1}{2}$ cups] cold syrup, pour over fruit. As the fruit tends to float, cover first with a piece of crumpled waxed paper or greaseproof paper before packing in polythene containers. Storage time: 12 months.	For serving alone or in puddings.

Other ways of freezing fruit.
1. *Open freezing*
   Arrange fruit on trays, freeze until firm, about 6 hours.
   Then pack in polythene bags. In this way each one is separate.
2. *Cover with sugar syrup*
   Pour over cold syrup of required strength, see page 42.
3. *Layering with sugar*
   Layer with castor sugar according to taste, about 4 oz. to one pound of fruit.
4. *Adding ascorbic acid*
   Peel peaches by blanching for 1 minute. Add ascorbic acid (Vitamin C) to prevent discolouration of peaches, apricots and pears, see page 44.

Plums	Choose ripe unblemished fruit. Covering with syrup is not recommended as the skins toughen on storage.	Wash if necessary. Dry. 1. Cut in half and remove stones. Pack in polythene containers. Cover with 45% syrup (see page 42). or 2. Leave whole. Pack in polythene bags. Storage time: 12 months.	1. For pies, crumbles and puddings. 2. For jam-making.
Raspberries	Pick fruit carefully in shallow baskets. Handle as little as possible.	Remove any stalks. Only wash, if absolutely necessary, and dry. 1. Open freeze (see page 47). Pack in polythene containers. or 2. Pack in small polythene containers enough for 1 portion. or 3. Purée fruit – add 6 oz. [¾ cup] sugar to each pint purée. Pack in small polythene containers or as ice cubes. Storage time: 12 months.	1. For serving straight with cream. As each fruit is separate, can be used for decoration. 2. Turn into individual dishes when partly thawed. 3. For flavouring ice cream, sorbets or mousses.
Rhubarb	Choose tender stalks picked early in the season. Can also be puréed.	Cut off green, wash and dry. Cut into ¾ in. lengths. 1. Pack into polythene bags or 2. Blanch fruit for 1 minute to retain colour and for easy packing. Pack in polythene containers. Storage time: 12 months.	1 and 2. Use for stewed rhubarb, pies, crumbles and puddings.
Strawberries	Choose firm, ripe fruit, small berries are best for freezing whole.	Remove stalks. Wash, if absolutely necessary, and dry. 1. Open freeze (see page 47). Pack in polythene containers or 2. Halve or slice fruit or leave small strawberries whole. Layer with sugar – 4 oz. [½ cup] to 1 lb. fruit in polythene containers or 3. Reduce fruit to a purée. Add 4 oz. [¾ cup] icing confectioners sugar to 1 pint [2½ cups] purée. Pack in small polythene containers. Storage time: 12 months.	1. For serving straight with cream or decorating sweet dishes. 2. For adding to fruit salad or making into puddings. 3. For flavouring ice cream or mousses.

Getting off to a Good Start

Family meals usually dispense with a first course, but many of the dishes included in this chapter are suitable for family snacks.

Artichoke Soup

This is one of the best winter soups. Artichokes are rather knobbly and difficult to peel but the resulting soup makes it well worth while.

1 lb. Jerusalem artichokes, peeled
1¼ pints (3 cups) water
1 chicken stock cube
½ teaspoon dried basil
1 bay leaf
2 sprigs of parsley
1 tablespoon (1¼T) parsley, chopped

1 onion, quartered
1 oz. (2T) butter
1 oz. (¼ cup) flour
½ pint (1¼ cups) milk
¼ pint (2/3 cup) single (light) cream
salt
pepper

Cut the artichokes in small pieces. Put in a pan with the water, stock cube, herbs and onion. Bring to boiling point, cover and simmer for about 45 minutes or until tender. Strain and remove the bay leaf and parsley. Purée the vegetables in a blender or put through a sieve. Heat the butter in a pan, blend in the flour and cook for 1 minute. Add the strained cooking liquor, milk and artichoke purée and bring to boiling point, stirring. Simmer for 5 minutes, then turn into a rigid container.
To freeze: cool, then cover, label and freeze.
To thaw: turn the frozen soup into a pan and thaw over a low heat, stirring frequently.
To serve: when the soup has boiled add the cream and adjust seasoning, then pour into bowls and sprinkle with parsley.
Serves 4

Potato and Leek Soup.

Potato and Leek Soup

1lb. potatoes, peeled
$\frac{3}{4}$ pint (2 cups) stock or $\frac{3}{4}$ pint
   (2 cups) water and a beef stock
   cube
3 leeks, sliced
salt
pepper
pinch of cayenne pepper
$\frac{1}{2}$ pint–1 pint ($1\frac{1}{4}$–$2\frac{1}{2}$ cups) milk
4 tablespoons (5T) single (light)
   cream
1 tablespoon ($1\frac{1}{4}$T) parsley, chopped

Cut the potatoes in small pieces. Put in a pan with the stock and cook 10 minutes. Wash the sliced leeks very thoroughly and add to the potatoes. Cook until tender, then sieve or reduce to a purée in a blender. Add the seasoning and cayenne pepper.
To freeze: turn into a rigid container, cover, label and freeze.
To thaw: turn the frozen soup into a pan and re-heat over a very low heat, stirring occasionally, or thaw at room temperature before heating. Thin down with milk to required consistency. Check seasoning.
To serve: add cream just before serving and decorate with chopped parsley.
Serves 4

Taramasalata

$\frac{1}{2}$ lb. smoked cod's roe
2 small slices white bread, de-crusted
2 tablespoons ($2\frac{1}{2}$T) milk
6 tablespoons ($7\frac{1}{2}$T) olive oil
2 tablespoons ($2\frac{1}{2}$T) lemon juice
freshly ground pepper

Remove skin from cod's roe. Place the roe in a mortar or bowl and pound with a pestle, or mash with a fork, until smooth. Soak the bread in the milk, then squeeze out as much of the milk as possible. Add the bread to the cod's roe and mash again. Add the oil a teaspoon at a time. Stir in the lemon juice and seasoning.
To freeze: put in a rigid polythene container, cover, label and freeze.
To thaw: thaw at room temperature for about 3 hours or in a refrigerator overnight.
To serve: serve with hot toast and butter as a starter.
Serves 4

French Onion Soup

This is a quick soup to make when you have fresh stock on hand. Alternatively you could use stock from the freezer.

2 tablespoons (2½T) oil
1 oz. (2T) butter
1 lb. onions, peeled and
    finely chopped
1 oz. (¼ cup) flour
1½ pints (4 cups) stock,
    preferably chicken or game

2 teaspoons tomato purée
salt
pepper
8 slices French bread, lightly
    toasted
1–2 oz. (¼–½ cup) Cheddar cheese,
    grated
sprigs of parsley

Heat the oil in a pan, add the butter then the onions and fry until beginning to brown. Blend in the flour and cook gently until brown then add the stock, tomato purée and seasoning. Bring to boiling point, stirring, and simmer, covered, 30–40 minutes.

To freeze: cool, turn into a rigid container. Cover, label and freeze.

To thaw: turn the frozen soup into a pan and thaw slowly over a low heat, stirring from time to time, or thaw at room temperature before re-heating.

To serve: sprinkle the slices of toasted bread with cheese. Pour the soup into an ovenproof tureen and arrange the slices of toast on top. Cook 425°F, Mark 7 until the cheese has melted and is just beginning to turn brown. Ladle the soup into individual bowls, floating the slices of toast on top of each bowl. Garnish with sprigs of parsley.
Serves 6

Smoked Mackerel Pâté

2 large smoked mackerel, or smoked
    trout, skinned and boned
3 oz. ($\frac{3}{8}$ cup) rich cream cheese
juice of $\frac{1}{2}$ lemon

10 oz. (1$\frac{1}{4}$ cups) butter, melted
salt
pepper
sprigs of parsley

Purée the mackerel in a blender, or mash well with a fork. Gradually add
the remaining ingredients and blend until smooth, or mash down the
mackerel with the cream cheese and add the other ingredients. Turn into
a 1 lb. loaf tin or terrine lined with foil.

To freeze: freeze 8 hours until firm. Turn out of the tin, wrap in foil, label
and return to freezer.

To thaw: thaw for about 8 hours in the refrigerator.

To serve: remove the foil and decorate with parsley sprigs. Serve with
hot toast and butter.

Serves 6

Scallops Mornay

These are delicious. If liked, pipe a border of mashed potato round the edge of shells before filling with the scallops in sauce.

8 scallops
8 tablespoons (½ cup) dry white wine
1 oz. (2T) butter
1 oz. (¼ cup) flour
½ pint (1¼ cups) milk
3 oz. (¾ cup) strong Cheddar cheese, grated

1 egg yolk
2 tablespoons (2½T) single (light) cream or top of the milk
salt
pepper

Remove the scallops from their shells. Wash thoroughly, removing beards and black parts. Put in a pan and simmer gently in the wine for 10 minutes. Make a roux with the butter and flour, blend in the milk and bring to boiling point, stirring. Simmer for 2 minutes. Remove the scallops from the pan, and boil the wine until reduced to 1 tablespoon (1¼T). Add the wine to the sauce with most of the grated cheese. Heat gently until smooth. Mix together the egg yolk and cream. Add to the sauce. Season, reheat, but do not boil.

Put little sauce in 4 deep scallop shells. Cut each scallop in several pieces, arrange in shells. Pour over the remaining sauce. Sprinkle with the remaining cheese.

To freeze: Pack each shell into a polythene bag. Open freeze (see page 47) if a border of piped potato has been done. Seal and label.

To thaw: cook gently under the grill for about 20 minutes. Turn up grill to brown for last 5 minutes.

To serve: serve hot.

Serves 4

Farmhouse Pâté

This is a rich, coarse pâté. Make sure to wrap it in double foil, then a polythene bag, as it could easily flavour other foods.

2 rashers (slices) streaky
   bacon, rinded
1 bay leaf
4 oz. (2 cups) fresh (soft)
   white breadcrumbs
1 egg, beaten
5 tablespoons (6¼ T) port
¼ lb. belly pork, in strips
½ lb. smoked bacon trimmings

½ lb. pig's liver
½ lb. chicken's liver
1 garlic clove, crushed
¼ teaspoon dried thyme
¼ teaspoon dried mixed herbs
½ teaspoon ground mace or
   nutmeg
1½ teaspoons salt
⅛ teaspoon pepper

Well grease a 2 pint (5 cup) terrine or loaf tin. Flatten and stretch the streaky bacon rashers with the blade of a knife on a board. Put the bay leaf in the centre of terrine, cover with the bacon rashers. Mix together the breadcrumbs, egg and port. Mince the belly pork with the bacon trimmings and liver. Add the garlic, herbs, mace and seasoning to the minced mixture, then add the egg mixture and mix well. Turn into the prepared terrine. Cover with foil, then a lid. Stand the terrine, with crumpled foil or a wire rack underneath to prevent bottom of the pâté from over-baking, in a large meat tin filled with hot water. Bake 325°F, Mark 3 for 2 hours.

To freeze: cool completely, then turn out and wrap in a double thickness of foil. Put in a polythene bag, seal, label and freeze.

To thaw: thaw in a refrigerator overnight or for 6 hours at room temperature.

To serve: serve as a starter with french bread or toast and butter.

Serves 6

Quick Pâté

Pâté is a great standby. This one is a smooth pâté. The last cuts make a good sandwich filling.

5 rashers (slices) streaky
   bacon, rinded
1 egg
4 oz. (2 cups) crustless bread
4 tablespoons (5T) dry sherry
½ lb. chicken's liver
½ garlic clove
½ lb. pig's liver

1½ teaspoons salt
⅛ teaspoon pepper
¼ teaspoon ground nutmeg
¼ teaspoon ground cloves
½ teaspoon dried mixed herbs
¼ lb. bacon trimmings, in
   small pieces
4 oz. (8T) lard, melted

Stretch the 5 rashers of streaky bacon with back of a knife on a board then
use to line the base and sides of a 2 pint (5 cup) loaf tin or deep pie dish.
Put the egg in a blender with the bread, broken in small pieces, and the
sherry and chicken livers. Reduce the mixture to a pulp in the blender,
then pour into a bowl. Put the remaining ingredients, except the lard,
in a blender and reduce to a pulp. Mix with the first mixture and stir in the
melted lard. Pour pâté into the tin or pie dish and cover tightly with foil.
Place in a meat tin half filled with warm water and cook at 325°F, Mark 3
for 2 hours.
To freeze : cool completely, turn out of the tin and wrap in a double
thickness of foil. Label and freeze.
To thaw : thaw at room temperature for 6 hours.
To serve : serve with hot toast and butter.
Serves 4

Chilled Melon Balls

*When melons are cheapest and at their best prepare these and use for
adding to shelled prawns and grapefruit wedges for a fruit cocktail. Or add to
fresh fruit salad.*

1 ripe melon, about 2 lb.

4 oz. (½ cup) castor
   (super fine) sugar

Cut the melon in half and discard pips. Scoop out the flesh in balls, using a small potato scoop. If you do not have a scoop cut the melon flesh in $\frac{1}{2}$ in. cubes. Mix with sugar. Divide between 4 suitable containers.
To freeze: cover, label and freeze.
To thaw: thaw overnight in a refrigerator or at room temperature for 3 hours.
To serve: serve as part of a fruit cocktail or fruit salad.

Melon Cocktail

1 small ripe melon
2 tablespoons ($2\frac{1}{2}$ T) lime
   juice cordial

$\frac{1}{4}$ pint ($\frac{2}{3}$ cup) sweet
   white wine
4 sprigs of mint

Halve the melon then remove and discard seeds. Peel the melon halves and discard skin. Cut the flesh in $\frac{1}{2}$ in. cubes, turn into a rigid container and mix in the lime juice and wine.
To freeze: cover, label and freeze.
To thaw: thaw overnight in a refrigerator.
To serve: divide between 4 glasses and top each with a sprig of mint.
Serves 4

American Mustard Dip

An easy dish to make. Ideal for a party or try using it as a sandwich filler.

8 oz. (1 cup) rich cream cheese
4 tablespoons (5T) mango chutney,
   chopped

$\frac{1}{4}$ teaspoon dry mustard
1 teaspoon curry powder

Mix together all the ingredients. Turn into a rigid container.
To freeze: cover, label and freeze.
To thaw: thaw in a refrigerator for 8 hours.
To serve: serve as a dip with crisps or sliced frankfurters.
Serves 6

Canelloni on Savoury Spinach

8 cannelloni pasta 'tubes'
½ quantity Ragu Bolognese sauce
   (see page 74)
Cheese sauce:
1 oz. (2T) butter
1 oz. (¼ cup) flour
½ pint (1¼ cups) milk

11 oz. packet (package)
   from leaf spinach

2 oz. (½ cup) Cheddar cheese, grated
½ teaspoon made mustard
salt, pepper

Cook the cannelloni in boiling, salted water for 10 minutes until just tender. Drain and rinse with cold water. Fill with the Ragu Bolognese mixture, using a teaspoon. Cook the spinach according to the directions on the packet (package). Place in a shallow foil container with the cannelloni on top.
Melt the butter for the sauce in a pan, blend in the flour and cook for 1 minute. Stir in the milk and bring to boiling point, stirring. Simmer for 2 minutes. Add the remaining ingredients then pour over cannelloni.
To freeze: cover with foil, seal, label and freeze.
To thaw: cook at 400°F, Mark 6 for 40 minutes until golden brown.
To serve: serve hot, with a green salad.
Serves 4

Ratatouille

2 large green peppers, seeded
2 oz. (4T) butter
2 medium onions, coarsely sliced
2 small aubergines (egg plants)
   in ¼ inch slices

½ lb. tomatoes, skinned,
   quartered and seeded
5 tablespoons (6¼ T) dry white wine
salt
pepper

Cut the green peppers in ½ inch strips. Heat the butter in a pan, add the peppers and onions. Fry for about 5 minutes or until the onion is soft and a pale golden brown. Add the aubergines (egg plants) and tomatoes with the wine to the pan. Cook for 5 minutes. Add seasoning to taste.
To freeze: cool, turn into a polythene bag, seal, label and freeze.
To thaw: thaw slowly in a non-stick pan over a low heat or in the oven at 325°F, Mark 3 for about 30 minutes.
To serve: serve as a starter, or as a vegetable with grills (broiled meat) and chops.
Serves 4

The Heart
of the Meal

Main courses may be simple for family consumption or elaborate for the benefit of guests. In either case, the value to you of having a number of main dishes stowed away in the freezer is immense. If you have to leave the family for a short while, there is no need to spend the whole of the day before preparing meals for your absence. A freezer really makes it possible to plan how and when to spend time in the kitchen. Recipes here include those for meat, fish, bacon and cheese dishes.

A word about cooking dishes straight from the freezer. This can be done and I have suggested it in most cases. If you prefer, as I do, to get food out of the freezer the day before then thaw it in the refrigerator overnight slowly – it saves fuel this way too. Remember to cut the cooking times as the food will be cold, not frozen, when it goes into the oven.

Pizza

½ oz. (1 T) butter
1 small onion, chopped
8 oz. can tomatoes
salt, pepper

½ teaspoon dried oregano
2 oz. Gruyère or Emmenthal cheese
6 anchovy fillets
8 black olives.

Cut off and weigh 4 oz. of the risen dough from the basic recipe (see page 112).

Melt the butter in a pan, add the onion and fry gently for 5 minutes. Add the tomatoes, salt and pepper and simmer, uncovered, for 15 minutes. The mixture should be thick. Cool. Roll the dough into an 8 in. circle and place in well-greased 8 in. sandwich tin. Spoon the tomato mixture over the top. Sprinkle with oregano. Cut the cheese into thin slices and place on top of mixture. Cut the anchovy fillets in half lengthways and arrange in a lattice design on top. Place olives between the lattice. Place inside a large, oiled polythene bag until the dough comes almost to top of the tin. Bake at 450°F, Mark 8 for 20–25 minutes.

To freeze: wrap the cooled pizza in a polythene bag or foil, seal, label and freeze. Store up to 2 months.

To thaw: unwrap and place frozen in the oven. Bake at 400°F, Mark 6 for 20 minutes.

Or:

prepare pizza up to covering top with tomato mixture. Open freeze in tin, then remove from tin, wrap in foil and return to freezer. Store up to 3 months.

To thaw: unwrap, place oregano, cheese, etc. on top and bake at 450°F, Mark 8 for 30–35 minutes.

To serve: serve hot, with a salad.

Serves 2–4

Alternative toppings for tomato mixture:

1. Sprinkle the tomato with thyme and arrange 4 rashers of rinded streaky bacon and 4 button mushrooms on top. Cover with thin slices of cheese.

2. Sprinkle the tomato with basil. Arrange 4 sardines on top and slices of fresh tomato between. Decorate with black olives or capers.

3. Arrange 2 slices of ham, cut in strips, on top. Sprinkle with 1½ oz. (scant ½ cup) grated Cheddar-type cheese and decorate with prunes, pickled walnuts or gherkins instead of olives.

Smoked Haddock Fish Cakes

1½ lb. old potatoes, peeled
salt
1½ lb. smoked haddock fillets
½ pint (1¼ cups) water
Sauce:
½ oz. (1T) butter
½ oz. (1/8 cup) flour
For finishing:
1 egg, beaten

¼ pint (2/3 cup) milk
2 tablespoons (2½T) parsley,
  chopped
pepper
1 teaspoon made mustard
¼ pint (2/3 cup) fish liquor

dried breadcrumbs

Cook the potatoes in boiling, salted water until tender. Drain and mash
until smooth. Put the fish in a large shallow pan with the water and milk.
Cover and simmer for 15 to 20 minutes, or until fish flakes easily when
touched. Remove from the pan, discarding skin and bones, turn into a bowl
and mash finely. Blend in the potato, parsley, pepper and mustard. Add
more salt if necessary but do not make mixture too salty.
Sauce: Boil the liquor that is left in the pan until just over ¼ pint (2/3 cup)
is left. Melt the butter for the sauce in a pan, blend in the flour and cook
for 1 minute. Add the fish liquor, bring to boiling point and simmer for
2 minutes.
Use as much of the sauce as necessary to bind the potato and fish mixture
together. Divide into 12 equal portions, then shape into flat, round cakes
on a floured board. Brush with beaten egg and then coat with breadcrumbs.
To freeze: put in a polythene bag or rigid container, seal, label and freeze.
To thaw: thaw in a refrigerator for 1 hour. Fry in deep fat or oil until
golden brown.
To serve: drain on kitchen paper and serve hot.
Serves 6

Sole à la Bonne Femme

8 fillets of sole
$\frac{1}{4}$ pint (2/3 cup) fish stock made from
    fish skin and bones and $\frac{1}{2}$ pint
    ($1\frac{1}{4}$ cups) water
Sauce:
2 oz. ($\frac{1}{2}$ cup) mushrooms,
    thinly sliced
$1\frac{1}{2}$ oz. (3T) butter
1 oz. ($\frac{1}{4}$ cup) flour
salt

Salt
pepper
$\frac{1}{4}$ pint (2/3 cup) dry white wine
1 teaspoon lemon juice

pepper
8 fl. oz. (1 cup) liquor in
    which fish was cooked
5 tablespoons ($6\frac{1}{4}$T) single (light)
    cream

Prepare the fish stock. Fold under both ends of each fillet to make a neat shape. Arrange in a shallow ovenproof dish and pour over the fish stock wine and lemon juice. Cover and cook 325°F, Mark 3 for 20–25 minutes or until the flesh is white and flakes easily. Drain the fillets, reserving liquor. Arrange the fillets in a shallow foil dish.

Sauce: Fry the mushrooms in $\frac{1}{2}$ oz. (1T) butter for 3 minutes. Remove from the pan. Melt the remaining butter in a pan, blend in the flour, then stir in liquor in which the fish was cooked and bring to boiling point, stirring. Simmer for 2–3 minutes. Add most of the mushrooms with the cream and more seasoning if necessary. Coat the fish fillets with the sauce and scatter the remaining mushrooms on top.

To freeze: cool, cover with foil, label and freeze.

To thaw: do not remove foil. Re-heat at 300°F, Mark 2 for about 30 minutes or until hot.

To serve: serve hot.

Serves 4

Bacon and Onion Quiche

4 oz. shortcrust pastry made
   with 4 oz. (1 cup) flour, etc.
   (see page 100)
1 small onion, finely chopped
$\frac{1}{2}$ oz. (1 T) butter

$\frac{1}{4}$ lb. bacon, rinded and chopped
1 egg
salt, pepper
$\frac{1}{4}$ pint (2/3 cup) single (light) cream
2 tomatoes, sliced

Use the pastry to line a 7 in. flan ring placed on a baking tray. Chill in
a refrigerator for 10 minutes then bake 'blind' 425°F, Mark 7 for 15 minutes.
Fry the onion in butter until soft but not coloured. Add the bacon and
fry until golden brown. Blend together the egg, seasoning and cream.
Remove the baking beans and greaseproof paper, or foil, from flan case.
Put the bacon and onion in the flan case. Strain the egg mixture on top.
Arrange tomato slices round edge. Cook at 350°F, Mark 4 for 35 minutes
or until filling is set.
To freeze: cool, pack in polythene bag, seal, label and freeze.
To thaw: cook at 350°F, Mark 4 for about 30 minutes.
To serve: serve hot with a green salad.
Variations: instead of bacon or onion add 4 oz. (1 cup) grated cheese,
prawns and chopped chives.
Serves 4

Bacon and Onion Quiche.

Sausage Rolls

Making this large amount at a time means that you can just dive into the polythene bag and take out as many as you like if guests arrive unexpectedly.

shortcrust pastry made with
    12 oz. (3 cups) plain (all-
    purpose) flour,
    6 oz. ($\frac{3}{4}$ cup) fat, etc.

1 lb. pork sausage meat
milk for glazing

Roll out the pastry to 4 strips, each 16 by 3 in. Roll out the sausage meat on a floured table to make 4 'worms' each 16 in long. Place one on each strip of pastry. Fold over the pastry, brush the edges with milk and seal firmly. Cut each in 8 sausage rolls.

Place on a baking tray and make 2 or 3 slashes with a sharp knife on top of each sausage roll. Brush with milk and bake at 425°F, Mark 7 for about 25 minutes until pale golden brown.

To freeze: cool on a wire rack then pack in polythene bags. Seal, label and freeze.

To thaw: place frozen sausage rolls on baking tray and re-heat at 425°F, Mark 7 for about 15 minutes.

To serve: serve hot.

Makes 32

Variations: add 1 teaspoon dried mixed herbs to sausage meat before shaping.

Boeuf Bourguignonne

1 oz. (2T) lard or bacon fat
6 rashers streaky bacon,
rinded and chopped
1$\frac{1}{2}$ lb. chuck (shoulder) steak,
    in 1$\frac{1}{2}$ inch cubes
1 tablespoon (1$\frac{1}{4}$T) flour
$\frac{1}{2}$ pint (1$\frac{1}{4}$ cups) stock or
    $\frac{1}{2}$ pint (1$\frac{1}{4}$ cups) water and
    a beef stock cube

$\frac{1}{4}$ pint (2/3 cup) cheap
    burgundy
1 bay leaf
$\frac{1}{2}$ teaspoon dried mixed
    herbs
sprig of parsley
$\frac{1}{2}$ teaspoon salt
1/8 teaspoon pepper
8 baby onions, peeled

Melt the lard or bacon fat in a fairly large pan. Add the bacon and fry until it begins to brown. Put the bacon in a 3 pint (7½ cup) ovenproof casserole. Brown steak in the fat remaining in the pan then add to the bacon in casserole. Pour away most of the fat in the pan, leaving about 2 tablespoons (2½T). Blend in the flour and cook until browned. Add all the remaining ingredients, except onions, and bring to boiling point, stirring. Simmer for 2 minutes then pour over meat. Cover and cook at 325°F, Mark 3 for 1½ hours. Add onions and cook further 30 minutes.
To freeze: turn into a rigid container, cool, cover, label and freeze.
To thaw: turn into an ovenproof, preferably non-stick, casserole. Cover and re-heat at 325°F, Mark 3 for about 40 minutes, stirring occasionally.
To serve: adjust seasoning if necessary and serve with boiled potatoes or noodles and a green vegetable.
Serves 4

Beef Stroganoff

1½ lb. fillet or rump steak
2½ oz. (5T) butter
1 large onion, chopped
4 oz. (1 cup) small mushrooms, sliced
2 tomatoes, skinned, pipped and
  chopped

1 tablespoon (1¼T) oil
2 × 5 oz. cartons (1¼ cups)
  soured cream
salt
pepper

Cut the steaks in strips about 2 in. long, ½ in. wide and ¼ in. thick. Melt 1 oz. (2T) butter in a pan, add the onion and fry until soft. Remove from the pan and add ½ oz. (1T) butter to the pan with mushrooms. Cook for 2 minutes, then add the tomato and cook for a further 2 minutes. Remove the mushrooms and tomatoes from the pan and add to the onion. Heat the remaining butter in a pan with the oil. Add half of the steak and fry for about 4 minutes until just cooked. Remove from the pan, then repeat with the remaining steak.
To freeze: put the vegetables and steak in a rigid container, cover, label and freeze.
To thaw: put the steak mixture in a pan and re-heat over low heat until piping hot, add soured cream. Add seasoning and bring just to simmering point.
To serve: serve hot.
Serves 4

Steak and Kidney Pies

$\frac{3}{4}$ lb. stewing steak, in $\frac{1}{2}$ in. cubes

$\frac{1}{4}$ lb. ox kidney, in $\frac{1}{2}$ in. cubes

2 tablespoons ($2\frac{1}{2}$ T), seasoned flour

1 oz. (2T) lard

1 large onion, finely chopped

$\frac{1}{2}$ pint ($1\frac{1}{4}$ cups) beef stock or $\frac{1}{2}$ pint ($1\frac{1}{4}$ cups) water and a beef stock cube

salt

pepper

Pastry:

12 oz. shortcrust pastry (see page 100) made with 12 oz. (3 cups) plain flour, etc.

milk or beaten egg for glazing

Toss the meat in the seasoned flour. Heat the lard in a pan, add the onion and fry for 2–3 minutes. Add the meat and fry until browned. Stir in the stock and seasoning and bring to boiling point. Cover and simmer for about 2 hours until the meat is tender. Cool.

Pastry: Roll out two-thirds of the pastry and cut in six $5\frac{1}{2}$ in. circles. Use the pastry to line 4 in. diameter patty tins. Roll out the remaining pastry and cut six 4 in. circles for lids. Divide the filling between the patty tins. Dampen the pastry edges and cover with lids. Knock up the edges and flute. Make a hole in centre of each pie. Roll out pastry trimmings and cut three leaves to decorate each pie. Glaze with beaten egg or milk. Bake at 400°F, Mark 6 for 25–30 minutes. Cool.

To freeze: wrap the cooled pies individually in a double layer of foil, label and freeze. Store up to 3–4 months.

To thaw: unwrap and leave at room temperature for 2–3 hours, then re-heat at 350°F, Mark 4 for about 20 minutes.

To serve: serve hot with vegetables.

Serves 6

Steak and Kidney Pies.

Large Steak, Kidney and Mushroom Pie

1¼ lb. stewing steak, in 1 in. pieces
¾ lb. ox kidney, in 1 in. pieces
1 oz. (¼ cup) flour
1½ oz. (3T) lard or dripping
2 onions, chopped
½ pint (1¼ cups) water

1 beef stock cube
1 teaspoon Worcestershire sauce
1 teaspoon salt
pinch of pepper
1 drop Tabasco
¼ lb. mushrooms (1 cup), sliced
½ lb. frozen puff pastry, thawed

Put the meat in a polythene bag with the kidney and flour and toss until coated. Melt the lard in a pan, add the meat and onions and fry until browned, stirring frequently. Add any remaining flour from tossing the meat. Add the remaining ingredients, except the mushrooms and pastry. Bring to boiling point, cover and simmer gently for 1½ hours. Stir the mushrooms into the meat mixture, check seasoning and then put in a 2½ pint (6 cup) foil pie dish.

To freeze: when cold, cover with the pastry, then cover with foil, label and freeze.

To thaw: brush with milk. Bake at 425°F, Mark 7 for 30 minutes. Lower to 350°F, Mark 4 for a further 20 minutes until the pastry is well risen and golden brown.

To serve: serve hot.

Serves 6

Beef Goulash

This is a good family dish for a cold day.

1½ lb. chuck (shoulder) or topside (hind shank) of beef
¼ lb. salt pork
½ oz. (1T) lard
1 large onion, chopped
1 oz. (¼ cup) flour
1 tablespoon (1¼T) paprika

1 pint (2½ cups) water
1 beef stock cube
6 small onions, peeled
6 small potatoes, peeled
6 small carrots, peeled
2 bayleaves
salt, pepper

Cut the beef in 1 in. pieces and the pork in $\frac{1}{2}$ in. pieces. Melt the lard in a pan and fry the pork slowly until brown. Remove from the pan and place in a $2\frac{1}{2}$ pint (6 cup) ovenproof dish. Add the beef and chopped onion to the pan. Cook quickly until brown, put in a casserole. Blend the flour with fat in a pan and cook for 1 minute. Stir in the paprika, then the water and stock cube. Bring to boiling point, stirring. Add the remaining ingredients, pour over meat and cook at 300°F, Mark 2 for 2 hours.

To freeze: cool, turn into a rigid container or polythene bag. Seal, label and freeze.

To thaw: turn into a casserole, preferably non-stick, cover and heat in a slow oven at 325°F, Mark 3 for about 40 minutes. Stir from time to time.

To serve: serve hot.

Variations: If you want this to go further add a large can of red kidney beans.

Serves 6

Beef Kromeskies

Kromeskies are an excellent way of using up the joint.

2 oz. (4T) butter

2 oz. ($\frac{1}{2}$ cup) flour

1 beef stock cube

$\frac{1}{2}$ pint ($1\frac{1}{4}$ cups) milk

$\frac{1}{2}$ lb. cooked, cold roast beef, finely chopped

For coating:

1 oz. ($\frac{1}{4}$ cup) flour

1 egg, beaten

1 egg, beaten

1 tablespoon ($1\frac{1}{4}$ T) parsley, chopped

salt

pepper

browned breadcrumbs

oil or fat for deep frying

Melt the butter in a pan, blend in the flour and cook for 1 minute. Crumble the stock cube in the milk, then blend in to a roux, bring to boiling point and simmer for 2 minutes, stirring well. Remove from the heat, and add the beef. Stir in the egg, parsley and seasoning, then leave until cold. Divide the mixture in 8 portions and shape into cylinder shapes. Coat each with flour, then egg and breadcrumbs.

To freeze: pack in a rigid container, cover, label and freeze.

To thaw: thaw overnight in a refrigerator. Heat the fat or oil, add the kromeskies and fry for about 4 minutes, until golden brown.

To serve: drain on kitchen paper and serve at once.

Variations: any cold meat may be used for kromeskies. Add a little chopped mint to lamb.

Serves 4

Lasagne al Forno

Ragu Bolognese Sauce:
2 rashers streaky bacon,
  rinded and chopped
1 lb. lean beef, minced
1 large onion, chopped
2 tablespoons (2½T) oil
2 sticks celery, chopped
1 garlic clove, crushed
¼ teaspoon dried mixed herbs
2 teaspoons salt
½ teaspoon sugar
⅛ teaspoon ground black pepper
5 tablespoons (6¼T) tomato purée
8 fl. oz. (1 cup) water
Bechamel Sauce:
¾ pint (2 cups) milk
1 bay leaf

2 peppercorns
1 blade mace
few parsley stalks
small carrot
piece of onion
1 oz. (2T) butter
1 oz. (¼ cup) flour
salt
pepper
Pasta
2 teaspoons oil
2 teaspoons salt
¼ lb. lasagne
4 oz. (1 cup) Gruyere cheese, grated
2 oz. (½ cup) Parmesan cheese,
grated

Fry the bacon, beef and onion for the Bolognese Sauce in the oil until
brown, stirring frequently. Add the remaining ingredients, cover and
simmer for 1 hour.

Bechamel Sauce: Heat the milk for the Bechamel Sauce in a pan with the
herbs, peppercorns and vegetables. Cover, and simmer gently for 10
minutes, then strain. Melt the butter in a pan, blend in the flour and cook
for 1 minute. Gradually add the milk and bring to boiling point, stirring.
Simmer for 2 minutes, add the seasoning, cover and keep hot.

In a large pan bring 4 pints (10 cups) water, with oil and salt from list of
pasta ingredients, to boil. Add the lasagne and boil for 8 minutes. Drain
in a colander, refresh with cold water, then arrange on a clean, damp tea
towel so the pieces do not stick together. Assemble the lasagne al forno in
three layers in a 3 pint (7½ cup) shallow ovenproof dish lined with foil
(see step-by-step picture opposite). Start with a layer of Bolognese Sauce,
then a layer of pasta, then a layer of Bechamel Sauce and Gruyere cheese.
Continue in this way, ending with layer of Bechamel Sauce. Sprinkle with
the remaining Gruyere and Parmesan.

To freeze: open freeze. Put in a polythene bag, seal, label and freeze.

To thaw: cook at 375°F, Mark 5 for about 1 hour, until golden brown.

To serve: serve with a green salad.

Serves 6

Lasagne. Layer pasta, sauces and cheese in foiled lined dish.
Open freeze in the shape of the dish.
Lift out of dish, label and put in polythene bag. Return to freezer.
Lasagne cooked straight from the freezer.

Frikadeller with Onion Sauce

These are delicious Danish meat balls.

$\frac{3}{4}$ lb. lean pork
$\frac{3}{4}$ lb. lean stewing beef
6 oz. (3 cups) fresh white
   breadcrumbs
1 onion, finely chopped
1$\frac{1}{2}$ teaspoons salt
Onion Sauce:
2 oz. (4T) dripping
4 onions, finely chopped
1 teaspoon castor (superfine) sugar
1$\frac{1}{2}$ oz. (3T) flour
1 pint (2$\frac{1}{2}$ cups) water

$\frac{1}{4}$ teaspoon pepper
$\frac{1}{4}$ teaspoon ground mace
1 rounded tablespoon (1$\frac{1}{4}$T)
   chopped parsley
1 egg, beaten
oil or fat for frying

1 beef stock cube
2 teaspoons tomato purée
few drops chilli sauce
salt
pepper

Cut the meat in strips, then mince finely. Mix with all other ingredients, except the egg. Blend in sufficient egg to bind the mixture together. Heat about 1 in. of oil or fat in a pan. Dip a tablespoon in the hot fat then gently drop rounded tablespoons of meat mixture into the fat. Fry on a medium heat for about 4 minutes on each side, until golden brown. Drain on kitchen paper, cool, then pack in a rigid container.

Onion Sauce: Melt the dripping in a pan, add the onions and fry slowly until soft and golden. Add the sugar and cook for a few minutes more. Blend in the flour and cook for 1 minute, then stir in the water. Bring to boiling point, stirring. Add the remaining ingredients and simmer for 10 minutes. Cool the sauce, then pour over frikadeller.

To freeze: seal, label and freeze.

To thaw: place in a heavy, preferably non-stick, casserole. Cover and cook at 350°F, Mark 4 for about 45 minutes, stirring from time to time.

To serve: check seasoning and serve hot.

Serves 6

Curried Shepherd's Pie

1 lb. potatoes
salt
$\frac{1}{2}$ oz. (1T) butter

1 oz. (2T) lard
1 lb. cooked meat, minced (ground)
1 onion, chopped

milk
salt
pepper

1 tablespoon ($1\frac{1}{4}$T) curry powder
$\frac{1}{2}$ pint ($1\frac{1}{4}$ cups) well-seasoned
   gravy

Boil the potatoes in salted water until very soft. Drain, then mash with
butter and milk until a smooth, spreading consistency is obtained.
Add the seasoning. Melt the lard in a pan, add meat and cook for 5 minutes.
Remove from the pan. Add the onion to the pan and cook until soft. Add
the curry powder and cook for 1 minute. Return the meat to the pan with
the gravy and mix well. Turn into a 2 pint (5 cup) pie dish. Cover with the
prepared potato.
To freeze: open freeze (see page 47) then cover with foil, label and return
to the freezer.
To thaw: uncover and cook at 350°F, Mark 4 for 1 hour or until golden
brown on top.
To serve: serve with creamed spinach.
Serves 4

Creamed Pork

2 tablespoons ($2\frac{1}{2}$T) oil
1 oz. (2T) butter
$1\frac{1}{2}$ lb. pork fillet, or boned loin
   of pork, in $1\frac{1}{2}$ in. pieces
1 onion, chopped
1 tablespoon ($1\frac{1}{4}$T) paprika pepper
1 tablespoon ($1\frac{1}{4}$T) flour
$\frac{1}{2}$ pint ($1\frac{1}{4}$ cups) stock or
   $\frac{1}{2}$ pint ($1\frac{1}{4}$ cups) water and
   a beef stock cube

5 tablespoons ($6\frac{1}{4}$T) dry sherry
1 teaspoon tomato purée
salt
pepper
6 oz. ($1\frac{1}{2}$ cups) small mushrooms
1 tablespoon ($1\frac{1}{4}$T) cornflour and
2 tablespoons ($2\frac{1}{2}$T) cold water,
   blended together
5 tablespoons ($6\frac{1}{4}$T) double (heavy)
   cream

Heat the oil in a pan. Add the butter and pork and fry quickly on both
sides until beginning to brown. Remove the pork from the pan and
drain on kitchen paper. Fry the onion in the pan with the paprika for
2 minutes. Blend in the flour and cook for 1 minute. Add the stock,
sherry and tomato purée. Bring to boiling point, stirring, then return
meat to pan. Add seasoning, cover and simmer for 30 minutes. Add the
mushrooms and blended cornflour to pan. Simmer until thickened.
To freeze: cool, turn into a rigid container, cover, label and freeze.
To thaw: put in an ovenproof, preferably non-stick, casserole. Cover and
re-heat at 325°F, Mark 3 for about 40 minutes, stirring occasionally.
To serve: add the cream and adjust seasoning just before serving.
Serves 4

Blanquette de Veau

$1\frac{1}{2}$ lb. boned shoulder veal, in $1\frac{1}{2}$ in. pieces
2 onions, quartered
2 large carrots, quartered
3 bay leaves
sprig of parsley
1 tablespoon ($1\frac{1}{4}$T) lemon juice

salt
pepper
2 pints (5 cups) water
6 oz. ($1\frac{1}{2}$ cups) small mushrooms
$1\frac{1}{2}$ oz. (3T) butter
$1\frac{1}{2}$ oz. (scant $\frac{1}{2}$ cup) flour
$\frac{1}{4}$ pint (2/3 cup) single (thin) cream

Put the veal in a pan, cover with cold water and bring to boiling point. Drain the veal and rinse off scum. Return the veal to the pan with the onions, carrots, herbs, lemon juice and seasoning. Add the 2 pints (5 cups) water, bring to boiling point. Cover and simmer for $1\frac{1}{2}$ hours or until tender.

Half an hour before the end of the cooking time add the mushrooms. Melt the butter in a pan, add the flour and cook for 1 minute. Put the veal and vegetables in a rigid container. Reduce the cooking liquor to 1 pint ($2\frac{1}{2}$ cups) by boiling rapidly. Add to the roux and simmer for 5 minutes. Check seasoning. Add cream and simmer for 1 more minute. Pour on a little of the sauce. Pour over the veal and vegetables.

To freeze: cool, cover, label and freeze.

To thaw: turn into a double saucepan or bowl over a pan of simmering water. Thaw slowly for about 45 minutes until piping hot. Do not allow to boil.

To serve: serve hot.

Blanquette de Veau.

Osso Buco

A rich Italian stew which is traditionally, and ideally, made from knuckle of veal, with the marrow in the bone carefully preserved in its entirety. If you have difficulty in getting knuckle, make this stew with shin or pie veal instead. It cannot then really be called osso buco, which means 'hollow bone' but it will be almost as good. The pale tomato-coloured chunky sauce is delicious and brings out the mild but full flavour of the veal.

2–2½ lb. knuckle veal or,
   if not available,
   1½ lb. boneless shin of veal
1 tablespoon (1¼ T) oil
½ oz. (1 T) butter
3 carrots, sliced
2 sticks celery, chopped
1 onion, chopped
1 garlic clove, crushed
Garnish:
grated rind of ½ lemon
2 tablespoons (2½ T) parsley,
   coarsely chopped

1 tablespoon (1¼ T) flour
¼ pint (2/3 cup) white Chianti
   or dry white wine
½ pint (1¼ cups) water
1 chicken stock cube
15 oz. can tomatoes
1 sprig of parsley
1 bay leaf
salt, pepper

½ garlic clove, crushed

Ask your butcher to saw the knuckle into 1½–2 in. sized chunks or, if using shin, cut into 1½ in. pieces. Heat the oil in a heavy frying pan, add the butter and fry half the meat at a time until golden brown. Take care not to let the marrow slip out of knuckle bone. Drain on kitchen paper then transfer to a 3 pint (7½ cup) ovenproof casserole. Fry the vegetables in the fat remaining in the pan for 5 minutes. Stir in the flour and cook until browned, then add the remaining ingredients. Bring to boiling point and pour over meat. Cover and cook at 325°F, Mark 3 for 3 hours.
To freeze: cool, turn into a rigid container. Cover, label and freeze.
To thaw: turn into an ovenproof, preferably non-stick, casserole. Cover and re-heat at 325°F, Mark 3 for about 40 minutes, stirring occasionally.
To serve: mix together the ingredients for garnish and sprinkle over Osso Buco.
Serves 4

Country Chicken Pie

½ lb. cooked chicken
¼ lb. cooked ham or bacon
2 oz. (4T) butter
4 oz. (1 cup) mushrooms
1 oz. (¼ cup) flour
½ pint (1¼ cups) milk
pinch of ground mace

salt
pepper
juice of ½ lemon
6 oz. rough puff pastry made with
   6 oz. (1½ cups) flour, 2 oz. (4T)
   butter, 2 oz. (4T) lard, etc.
beaten egg or milk for glazing

Cut the chicken and bacon in small pieces. Melt half of the butter in a pan, add the mushrooms and fry for 1 minute. Remove the mushrooms. Melt the remaining butter in the pan. Blend in the flour, and cook for 1 minute. Stir in the milk and bring to boiling point, stirring. Simmer for 2 minutes, add mace, seasoning and lemon juice. Add the chicken, bacon and mushrooms to sauce, mixing well. Allow to cool while preparing the pastry.

Turn mixture into 1½ pint (4 cup) ovenproof dish. Cover with the pastry. Decorate with pastry leaves.

To freeze: open freeze (see page 47) for 8 hours, to prevent 'leaves' being crushed. Put into a polythene bag, seal, label and freeze.

To thaw: brush with milk or egg blended with milk. Bake at 425°F, Mark 7 for 30 minutes. Lower oven to 350°F, Mark 4 for a further 20 minutes.

To serve: serve hot.

Variations: make same pie with cooked veal and ham. You could also use bought puff pastry instead of home-made.

Serves 4

Mild Curried Chicken

4 tablespoon (5T) oil
1 chicken, jointed or
    8 drumsticks
2 onions, chopped
1 oz. ($\frac{1}{4}$ cup) flour
1 tablespoon ($1\frac{1}{4}$T) curry powder
    or more if liked
$\frac{1}{2}$ pint ($1\frac{1}{4}$ cups) water

1 chicken stock cube
1 tablespoon ($1\frac{1}{4}$T) mango chutney
1 tablespoon ($1\frac{1}{4}$T) cherry jam
salt
pepper
1 oz. (1/6 cup) sultanas
    (seedless white raisins)
1 sweet apple, cored and chopped

Heat the oil in a pan, add chicken joints and fry until golden brown,
turning once. Take from the pan and remove skin and bones.
Add the onions to the oil remaining in the pan and fry slowly until soft.
Blend in the flour and curry powder and cook for 1 minute. Add the stock
gradually, then bring to boiling point, stirring. Simmer until the sauce has
thickened. Add the chutney and jam. Season with salt and pepper.
Replace the chicken in the pan, cover and simmer gently for 30 minutes
or until tender. Stir in the sultanas and apple and cook for a further
5 minutes.
To freeze: turn into a rigid container, seal, label and freeze.
To thaw: turn into a heavy, preferably non-stick, casserole. Cover and
re-heat at 325°F, Mark 3 for about 40 minutes, stirring from time to time.
To serve: serve with boiled rice, lemon wedges and side dishes, e.g.
bananas, sliced and sprinkled with lemon juice, dessicated coconut,
wedges or slices of hard boiled egg, fried poppadums, chopped cucumber
and tomato, mango chutney, and peanuts.
Variations: use either lamb or beef if preferred. Or make sauce only,
freeze. Thaw and re-heat when required and serve over hard-boiled eggs.
Serves 4

Cidered Chicken

1 lb. piece of boiling bacon
1 bay leaf
1 onion, quartered
3 lb. roasting chicken
1 onion, sliced
$\frac{1}{2}$ lb. carrots, peeled and
    sliced

4 sticks celery, chopped
$\frac{1}{2}$ teaspoon salt
$\frac{1}{4}$ pint (2/3 cup) dry cider
$1\frac{1}{2}$ pints (4 cups) water
$1\frac{1}{2}$ oz. (3T) butter
$1\frac{1}{2}$ oz. (3T) flour
pepper

Soak the bacon in cold water overnight. Place in a pan, cover with fresh water and add the bay leaf and quartered onion. Bring to boiling point, cover and simmer for 40 minutes.

Put the chicken and giblets in another pan with the vegetables, salt, cider and water. Cover and simmer for 40 minutes until tender, then remove from pan, saving stock and vegetables.

Cut the bacon in $\frac{1}{2}$ in. cubes, discard skin and fat. Cut the chicken in 1 in. pieces, discard skin and bone.

Make a roux with the butter and flour and cook for 1 minute. Blend in the strained chicken liquor and bring to boiling point. Check seasoning. Add the bacon, chicken and vegetables.

To freeze: turn into large foil or rigid polythene container. Cool, cover with foil, label and freeze.

To thaw: put in a heavy, preferably non-stick, casserole. Cover and re-heat at 325°F, Mark 3 for about 40 minutes. Stir from time to time.

To serve: serve hot.

Serves 8

Foiled Lamb in Barbecue Sauce

4 lamb cutlets, boned
1 oz. ($\frac{1}{4}$ cup) seasoned flour
1 oz. (2T) dripping
1 large onion, chopped
1 lb. tomatoes, skinned
    and quartered

1 garlic clove, crushed
$\frac{1}{4}$ teaspoon dried mixed herbs
salt
pepper

Roll up each cutlet neatly and secure with fine string. Toss the cutlets in seasoned flour. Heat the dripping in a frying pan, add cutlets and brown quickly, turning once. Remove cutlets from the pan and place each cutlet on a double thickness of foil, 10 in. square.

Add the onion to the pan and cook until soft. Blend in the remaining flour, cook for 1 minute. Add the tomatoes, garlic and herbs and simmer for 2 minutes. Check seasoning then spoon the sauce over cutlets. Wrap each cutlet firmly in foil.

To freeze: label each parcel and freeze.

To thaw: put parcels on a baking tray and cook at 325°F, Mark 3 for $1\frac{1}{4}$ hours.

To serve: serve straight from foil.

Serves 4

Paprika Lamb Goulash

1 oz. (2T) lard
2 lb. middle neck of lamb,
   cut in joints
1 onion, chopped
1 garlic clove, crushed
2 tablespoons ($2\frac{1}{2}$T) paprika
15 oz. can tomatoes

sprig of parsley
1 bay leaf
salt
pepper
$\frac{1}{2}$ teaspoon sugar
1 lb. small potatoes, peeled

Melt the lard in a pan. Add the lamb and brown for about 5 minutes, turning once. Remove the meat from the pan and put in a $2\frac{1}{2}$ pint (6 cup) casserole.

Fry the onion and garlic in the fat remaining in the pan until soft. Add the paprika and cook for 1 minute. Add the remaining ingredients, except potatoes. Bring to boiling point and pour over the meat. Cover and cook at 325°F, Mark 3 for 1 hour.

Remove parsley and bay leaf. Skim off any excess fat. Add the potatoes to the casserole, cover and cook for 30 minutes.

To freeze: turn into a rigid polythene container. Cool, cover, label and freeze.

To thaw: turn into an ovenproof, preferably non-stick, casserole. Cover and re-heat at 325°F, Mark 3 for about 40 minutes, stirring occasionally.

To serve: adjust seasoning and serve hot.

Serves 4

Lancashire Hot Pot

2 lb. middle neck of lamb
1 tablespoon ($1\frac{1}{4}$T) flour
salt, pepper
$1\frac{1}{2}$ lb. potatoes
$\frac{1}{2}$ lb. onions, sliced

2 lambs' kidneys, skinned, cored
   and quartered
$\frac{1}{4}$ lb. (1 cup) mushrooms, sliced
$\frac{3}{4}$ pint (2 cups) stock
$\frac{1}{2}$ oz. (1T) butter

Cut the lamb in even-sized chops and pieces. Mix together the flour and
seasoning and toss the meat in it. Peel the potatoes and cut in $\frac{1}{4}$ in. thick
slices. Put the meat, onion, kidneys and mushrooms in a casserole.
Arrange the potatoes on top. Pour on the stock. Dot with butter. Cover and
cook at 350°F, Mark 4 for about 2 hours.
To freeze: cool, pack in a rigid container, cover, label and freeze.
To thaw: turn into a casserole, potatoes on top, and cook at 350°F, Mark 4
for about 45 minutes. Uncover dish for last 30 minutes to brown potatoes.
To serve: serve hot.
Serves 4

Sherried Kidneys

$1\frac{1}{2}$ lb. sheep kidneys, skinned
3 oz. (6T) butter
1 large onion, chopped
1 oz. ($\frac{1}{4}$ cup) flour
5 tablespoons ($6\frac{1}{4}$T) dry sherry
$\frac{1}{2}$ pint ($1\frac{1}{4}$ cups) water
Garnish:
3 large slices white bread
oil for frying

1 beef stock cube
1 garlic clove, crushed
1 bay leaf
1 teaspoon salt
$\frac{1}{8}$ teaspoon pepper

1 tablespoon ($1\frac{1}{4}$T) parsley,
   chopped

Remove the cores from the kidneys and cut the kidneys in $\frac{1}{2}$ in. pieces.
Melt the butter in a pan, add the onions and fry gently until golden
brown. Add the kidneys to the pan and fry for 2 minutes on each side.
Remove the onion and kidneys from the pan.
Blend the flour with the fat remaining in pan and cook for 1 minute.
Stir in the sherry, water and stock cube and bring to boiling point.
Return the onion and kidneys to the pan with the remaining ingredients.
Cover and simmer gently for $\frac{1}{4}$ hour until tender. Remove the bay leaf.
Remove the crusts from the bread and cut each slice in 4 triangles. Fry in
the oil until golden brown, then drain on kitchen paper (paper towels).
To freeze: pack the kidney mixture and bread croûtes in separate rigid
containers. Cover, label and freeze.

To thaw: put the kidney mixture in a heavy, preferably non-stick, casserole. Cover and re-heat at 325°F, Mark 3 for about 40 minutes, stirring from time to time. Meanwhile thaw the bread croûtes in the warming drawer of the oven.

To serve: turn the kidney mixture onto a flat serving dish. Scatter the parsley on top and arrange croûtes round the edge.

Serves 6

Moussaka

2 lb. aubergines (eggplants), in ½ in. slices
7 tablespoons (8¾ T) salad oil
1 lb. raw shoulder lamb, minced (ground)
½ lb. onions, chopped
1 garlic clove, crushed
Cheese Sauce:
1 oz. (2 T) butter
1 oz. (¼ cup) flour
½ pint (1¼ cups) milk
4 oz. (1 cup) Emmenthal cheese, grated

1 oz. (¼ cup) flour
salt
pepper
15 oz. can tomatoes
¼ teaspoon mixed dried herbs
2 tablespoons (2½ T) parsley, chopped

½ teaspoon made mustard
salt
pepper

Sprinkle the aubergines (eggplants) with salt, leave for 30 minutes, then drain and dry with kitchen paper. Fry the aubergines (eggplants) in 6 tablespoons (7½ T) oil until brown. Remove from the pan, drain on kitchen paper.

Put the remaining oil in the pan with the minced (ground) lamb and fry until browned. Add the onion and garlic to pan and cook for 10 minutes. Blend in the flour, about 1 teaspoon salt, pepper, tomato juice, herbs and most of chopped parsley.

Butter a shallow 1½ pint (4 cup) ovenproof dish or line dish with foil (see Lasagne picture on page 75). Arrange the aubergines (eggplants) and meat mixture in layers, finishing with a layer of aubergine (eggplant).

Cheese Sauce: make a roux with the butter and flour for sauce. Blend in the milk, bring to boiling point, stirring, then simmer for 2 minutes. Add most of the cheese, mustard and seasonings. Pour over the aubergine (eggplant) slices. Sprinkle with the remaining cheese.

To freeze: put in a polythene bag, seal, label and freeze.

To thaw: cook at 400°F, Mark 6 for about 1 hour until golden brown.

To serve: serve with French bread and butter.

Serves 4

Braised Liver and Onions

1 lb. young ox's liver,
    thinly sliced
1 oz. (2T) lard or dripping
4 rashers bacon, rinded and
    roughly chopped
Garnish:
parsley, chopped

1 lb. onions, chopped
1 oz. ($\frac{1}{4}$ cup) flour
$\frac{1}{2}$ pint ($1\frac{1}{4}$ cups) water
1 beef stock cube
2 teaspoons salt
$\frac{1}{4}$ teaspoon pepper

Wash the liver in warm water then drain on kitchen paper. Remove any large tubes. Melt the lard in a pan and fry the bacon lightly. Remove from the pan. Add the onions to the pan and fry slowly until just beginning to brown. Blend in the flour and cook for 1 minute. Stir in the remaining ingredients. Bring to boiling point, stirring. Add the liver and bacon, cover and simmer for 30 minutes.
To freeze: cool, pack in polythene bag, seal, label and freeze.
To thaw: put in a bowl over a pan of simmering water. Cover with the lid. Stir frequently until piping hot, about 30 minutes.
To serve: serve hot with mashed potatoes and buttered cabbage.
Serves 4

Jugged Hare

1 hare, cut in neat pieces
2 oz. (4T) bacon fat
2 large onions, each stuck with
    2 cloves
1 stick celery, chopped
6 peppercorns
rind of $\frac{1}{2}$ lemon
Liaison:
2 oz. ($\frac{1}{4}$ cup) butter
Gravy:
$\frac{1}{4}$ pint ($\frac{2}{3}$ cup) port
Garnish:
Fried bread croûtes

pinch of cayenne pepper
1 sprig of thyme
1 bay leaf
2 sprigs of parsley
1 blade of mace
salt, pepper
2 pints (5 cups) water

2 oz. ($\frac{1}{2}$ cup) flour

1 tablespoon ($1\frac{1}{4}$ T) redcurrant jelly

parsley, chopped

It takes time to prepare and cook a hare, so do a couple at once and freeze in two or more containers. Freeze the fried bread croûtes separately to serve with the hare.

Fry the hare joints in the bacon fat in a large pan until browned. Put the joints in a large, heavy ovenproof casserole with the other ingredients. Cover tightly and cook at 325°F, Mark 3 for 2–3½ hours, depending on age of hare, until hare is tender.

Pour the gravy through a strainer into a pan and remove the vegetables, spices, lemon rind and herbs from the casserole.

Liaison: soften the butter for liaison in a small bowl, then blend in the flour to make a smooth paste. Add the kneaded butter in small pieces to the gravy, whisking until smooth. When all the kneaded butter has been added bring the gravy to boiling point and simmer until it has thickened, stirring constantly. Add the port and redcurrant jelly to the gravy and simmer gently until the jelly has dissolved. Adjust the seasoning if necessary.

To freeze: put hare joints into a rigid container, then pour over gravy. Cool, cover, label and freeze.

To thaw: put in a large, preferably non-stick, casserole. Cover and re-heat at 325°F, Mark 3 for about 40 minutes, stirring from time to time.

To serve: serve garnished with bread croûtes and chopped parsley.

Serves 6–10, depending on size of hare.

Casseroled Grouse

3 old grouse, plucked and
   drawn
1 oz. (2T) dripping
2 carrots, diced
1 small turnip, diced
1 large onion, chopped
3 rashers (slices) streaky bacon,
   chopped

¼ pint (2/3 cup) red wine
½ pint (1¼ cups) water
1 chicken stock cube
1 tablespoon (1¼T) redcurrant or
   damson jelly
juice of ½ lemon
1 teaspoon salt
⅛ teaspoon pepper

Halve the grouse and brown quickly in the hot dripping in a pan. Remove from the pan and put in a 3 pint (7½ cup) casserole.

Add the vegetables and bacon to pan, cook gently until golden. Add the remaining ingredients to pan, bring to boiling point, then pour over the grouse. Cover and cook at 300°F, Mark 2 for 2½ hours.

To freeze: cool, then turn into a large foil container or a polythene bag. Seal, label and freeze.

To thaw: turn into a heavy, preferably non-stick, casserole, and re-heat at 325°F, Mark 3 for about 40 minutes, stirring from time to time.

To serve: serve hot.

Variations: old pheasants can be cooked in this way too.

Serves 6

Cauliflower au Gratin

An easy supper dish. If the family have large appetites serve with fried bread croûtons (see page 30) and bacon rolls.

2 lb. cauliflower
1½ oz. (3T) butter
1½ oz. (3T) flour
¾ pint (2 cups) milk
3 oz. (¾ cup) Cheddar cheese, grated
salt

pepper
½ teaspoon made mustard
1 tablespoon (1¼T) Parmesan cheese, grated
2 tablespoons (2½T) dried breadcrumbs

Break the cauliflower into florets and cook in boiling, salted water until barely tender. Drain, reserving 4 tablespoons (5T) cooking liquor. Make a roux with the butter and flour, blend in the milk and bring to boiling point. Simmer for 2 minutes, then remove from heat. Add the Cheddar cheese, seasoning and mustard, and stir until the cheese has melted. Add the cauliflower and reserved liquor, mixing well.
To freeze: turn into a foil container. Mix together Parmesan and breadcrumbs and scatter on top. Cool, cover with foil, label and freeze.
To thaw: remove foil lid and re-heat at 400°F, Mark 6 for 30 minutes.
Variations: prepare leeks and chicory in this way too. Add a little sugar to the cooking water of chicory. It helps to take away the bitter taste.
Serves 6 as a starter or 4 as a main course.

Piped Duchesse Potatoes

1 lb. potatoes, peeled
1 egg yolk
1 oz. (2T) butter

salt
pepper
beaten egg for glazing

Cook the potatoes in boiling, salted water until tender, then drain and mash until smooth. Beat in the egg yolk, butter and seasoning.
Pipe in large rosettes on a greased baking tray, then brush with the beaten egg. Bake at 425°F, Mark 7 for about 10 minutes until just golden.
To freeze: cool then open freeze (see page 47). Remove from baking tray, and put in a polythene bag, seal, label and return to freezer.
To thaw: place, frozen, on baking tray and re-heat at 425°F, Mark 7 for about 25 minutes.
Serves 4

To Freeze Long Grain Rice

Cook refined long-grain rice in plenty of boiling, salted water until just tender. Rinse in plenty of cold water and drain well. Freeze in $\frac{1}{2}$ lb. in polythene bags.

To cook: plunge frozen rice into boiling, salted water. Bring back to the boil, simmer for 1 minute, then drain and serve.

Chicken Stock

Save chicken carcasses in your freezer until you have several, then use to make this chicken stock.

2 or 3 chicken carcasses	1 teaspoon dried mixed herbs
water	$\frac{1}{4}$ teaspoon ground mace
1 teaspoon salt	2 carrots, sliced
$\frac{1}{4}$ teaspoon pepper	2 onions, sliced
1 bay leaf	few bacon trimmings, if available

Break up the chicken carcasses roughly with a rolling pin, then put in a large pan with just sufficient water to cover and all the other ingredients. Cover and simmer for 1 hour. Strain the stock and leave to cool. Remove any flesh from the carcasses.

To freeze: pour the strained stock into a rigid container, cover, label and freeze. Put the chicken meat in a small polythene bag, seal, label and freeze. Transfer the stock to a polythene bag when frozen, so container can be used again.

To thaw: add the frozen stock to soups, casseroles, etc. as required. Add the chicken meat to soups, fricassées, etc.

Note: make beef stock in same way, using bones from the joint or with fresh bones from the butcher.

A Fine Finish

Pudding is a term which covers a multitude of dishes from a light, fluffy dessert to a good, stout, body-warming pudding. I have included a number of old favourites, some ever popular with my children, others which have proved to be great standbys when entertaining.

Ice Cream

This is the best ice-cream that I know – the coffee flavour is, I find, the most popular.

4 eggs, separated
4 oz. (¾ cup) icing (confectioners') sugar, sifted

½ pint (1¼ cups) double (heavy) cream

Whisk the egg yolks in a small bowl until well blended. In another, larger, bowl whisk the egg whites until stiff then whisk in the icing (confectioners') sugar a teaspoon at a time. Whisk the cream until it forms soft peaks, then fold into meringue mixture with egg yolks. Turn into a 2½ pint (6 cup) rigid container.
To freeze: cover, label and freeze.
To thaw: thaw at room temperature for 15 minutes.
To serve: serve in scoopfuls with sponge fingers or thin biscuits.

Variations:

Blackcurrant ice-cream: sieve $\frac{1}{2}$ lb. blackcurrants. Add purée to mixture with egg yolks.

Strawberry ice-cream: sieve $\frac{1}{2}$ lb. fresh or thawed frozen fruit and fold into mixture with few drops of red colouring before putting in freezer container.

Coffee ice-cream: add 2 tablespoons ($2\frac{1}{2}$T) strong coffee and 1 tablespoon ($1\frac{1}{4}$T) rum or brandy to mixture before freezing.

Chocolate ice-cream: mix 2 tablespoons ($2\frac{1}{2}$T) cocoa with 4 tablespoons (5T) cold milk, cook over low heat until piping hot, thinning down with little extra milk if necessary, cool and fold into mixture before freezing.

Serves 6–8

Iced Strawberry Soufflés

This is a fruit ice-cream served as individual iced soufflés. They look most impressive for a party.

$\frac{1}{2}$ pint ($1\frac{1}{4}$ cups) double (heavy) cream

$\frac{1}{4}$ pint ($\frac{2}{3}$ cup) single (light) cream

3 egg whites

To decorate:

$\frac{1}{4}$ pint ($\frac{2}{3}$ cup) double (heavy)

6 oz. ($\frac{3}{4}$ cup) castor (superfine) sugar

$\frac{1}{4}$ pint ($\frac{2}{3}$ cup) strawberry purée (see page 49)

1 tablespoon ($1\frac{1}{4}$T) lemon juice

Tie paper collars securely round the outside of 4 × $\frac{1}{4}$ pint ($\frac{2}{3}$ cup) soufflé dishes. The collars should be about 2 in. deeper than dishes. Put the creams in a bowl and whisk until mixture forms soft peaks. In another bowl whisk the egg whites until they form stiff peaks, then whisk in the sugar a tablespoon at a time, whisking well after each addition. Fold the strawberry purée, whipped cream and lemon juice into the egg whites. Divide the mixture between the soufflé dishes. Put on a small tray or baking dish.

To freeze: open freeze (see page 47) then put each in a polythene bag, seal, label and return to freezer.

To thaw: remove from polythene bags and leave for 10 minutes at room temperature before removing paper collars.

To serve: decorate with whipped cream just before serving.

Serves 4

Orange Sorbet

3 oz. ($\frac{3}{8}$ cup) castor (superfine)
  sugar
$\frac{1}{2}$ pint (1$\frac{1}{4}$ cups) water

6 fl. oz. can ($\frac{3}{4}$ cup) concentrated
  frozen orange juice, undiluted
1 egg white

Put the sugar and water into a pan and heat slowly until the sugar has
dissolved. Allow the syrup to cool. Add the orange juice to the sugar
syrup and blend together.
Pour into a 1 pint (2$\frac{1}{2}$ cup) shallow rigid container. Cover and freeze
for 30 minutes. Turn into a bowl and mash with a fork until there are no
large pieces. Fold in stiffly whisked egg white.
To freeze: return to the container, cover and freeze until needed.
To thaw: thaw in a refrigerator for 30 minutes before serving.
To serve: serve in scoopfuls made with an ice-cream scoop or dessertspoon.
For a special occasion decorate with fresh orange wedges and mint sprigs.
Serves 4

Pineapple Ice Cream

1 medium-size fresh
  pineapple
juice of 1$\frac{1}{2}$ lemons
$\frac{1}{4}$ pint ($\frac{1}{2}$ cup) water

6 oz. ($\frac{3}{4}$ cup) castor (superfine)
  sugar
$\frac{1}{2}$ pint (1$\frac{1}{4}$ cups) double (heavy)
  cream, lightly whipped

Cut the pineapple in half lengthways, and cut out the hard core down the
centre of each side. Keep the pineapple shells. With a grapefruit knife
or a sharply pointed spoon, scoop out all flesh and chop finely, saving the
juice. Mix the chopped pineapple, juice, and lemon juice together.
Dissolve the sugar with the water in a pan over low heat, then cool.
Add the sugar syrup to the pineapple and pour into a rigid container.
To freeze: cover and freeze until almost set then turn mixture into a
bowl and whisk until broken up and light. Fold in the cream and return
to container. Cover, label and freeze until required.
To thaw: thaw at room temperature for 15 minutes.
To serve: scoop out ice-cream with a metal spoon that has been dipped
in boiling water. Serve in pineapple shells.
Note: a blender speeds up this recipe. Put the pineapple flesh, any juice
and lemon juice in a blender, switch on for 2 minutes, then add cooled
sugar syrup.
Serves 6

Pineapple ice cream is deliciously refreshing. The pineapple flesh is puréed or finely chopped, then blended with
sugar syrup and cream.

Serve in the pineapple shell.

Iced Lemon Soufflés

grated rind and juice of
3 lemons
3 large eggs, separated
5 oz. ($\frac{5}{8}$ cup) castor (superfine)
sugar
Decoration:
$\frac{1}{4}$ pint ($\frac{2}{3}$ cup) double (heavy)
cream, lightly whipped

$\frac{1}{2}$ oz. (4 teaspoons) (5 American
teaspoons) powdered gelatine
3 tablespoons ($3\frac{3}{4}$T) cold water
$\frac{1}{4}$ pint ($\frac{2}{3}$ cup) double (heavy)
cream, lightly whipped

Place a collar of kitchen foil, 1 in. deeper than each dish, round outside
of 6 individual soufflé dishes and secure firmly with freezer tape.
(Dishes should be about $\frac{1}{4}$ pint – $\frac{2}{3}$ cup – capacity.)
Whisk the lemon rind, juice, egg yolks and sugar in a basin over a pan
of hot water until mixture begins to thicken.
Dissolve the gelatine with water in a cup placed in a pan of simmering
water. Stir the dissolved gelatine into the lemon mixture, then leave in a
cool place until it begins to thicken, stirring occasionally. Fold the cream
into mixture, followed by stiffly whisked egg whites. Turn mixture into
prepared dishes.
To freeze: open freeze (see page 47) then place each soufflé in an individual
polythene bag, seal, label and return to freezer.
To thaw: remove polythene bags and thaw at room temperature for about
3 hours.
To serve: carefully remove foil collars and decorate each soufflé with a
whirl of cream.
Serves 6

Iced Lemon Syllabub Cream

*Freeze in yoghurt or cream cartons. Turn out to serve and top with slices
of fresh lemon.*

1 large lemon
5 tablespoons ($6\frac{1}{4}$T) fairly
sweet sherry
2 tablespoons ($2\frac{1}{2}$T) brandy

2 oz. ($\frac{1}{4}$ cup) castor (superfine)
sugar
$\frac{1}{2}$ pint ($1\frac{1}{4}$ cups) double (heavy)
cream

Put the finely grated lemon rind in a bowl with the lemon juice. Add the sherry, brandy and sugar. Stir until the sugar has dissolved. Pour in the cream and whisk the mixture until it will form soft peaks when the whisk is lifted out. Pour in to 4 yoghurt or cream cartons.

To freeze: cover with foil, label and freeze.

To thaw: dip each carton in hot water for 2 seconds then turn out the syllabub cream on to individual plates 10 minutes before serving.

To serve: top each with a slice of fresh lemon and serve at once.

Serves 4

Austrian Rum Dessert Cake

3 eggs
3 oz. ($\frac{3}{8}$ cup) castor
   (superfine) sugar
2 oz. ($\frac{1}{2}$ cup) self-raising flour
1 oz. ($\frac{1}{4}$ cup) cocoa
Decoration:
chocolate curls

2 tablespoons ($2\frac{1}{2}$ T) corn oil
$\frac{1}{2}$ pint ($1\frac{1}{4}$ cups) double (heavy)
   cream, lightly whipped
3 tablespoons ($3\frac{3}{4}$ T) rum

Line and grease a deep 7 in. diameter cake tin.

Whisk the eggs and sugar together in a bowl over a pan of hot water until pale and thick. Remove from the heat. Sift the flour and cocoa together and fold into the egg mixture with the corn oil. Turn into prepared tin and bake at 350°F, Mark 4 for about 40 minutes or until the centre of sponge springs back into place when lightly pressed. Remove from the tin and leave to cool before cutting in half. Mix the cream and rum together and use half to sandwich the sponge together. Spread the remaining cream on top of the cake.

To freeze: open freeze (see page 47) then wrap in foil, label and return to freezer.

To thaw: remove foil, put cake on serving dish and thaw at room temperature for about 3 hours.

To serve: decorate with chocolate curls (see page 108).

Serves 4–6

Oranges in Liqueur

8 large Jaffa oranges
4 oz. ($\frac{1}{2}$ cup) castor (superfine)
   sugar

4 tablespoons (5T) liqueur, e.g.
   Cointreau, Curaçao or Grand
   Marnier

Finely grate the rind of two oranges. Using a sharp knife, cut the peel from all the oranges so that the pith is completely removed. Cut the oranges in thin slices. Divide the oranges between 2 rigid containers. Sprinkle with the grated rind and sugar.
To freeze: cover, label and freeze.
To thaw: thaw at room temperature for 3 to 4 hours.
To serve: add the liqueur just before serving.
For two lots to serve 4

Fresh Fruit Salad

4 oz. ($\frac{1}{2}$ cup) castor (superfine)
   sugar
8 tablespoons ($\frac{1}{2}$ cup) water
juice of $\frac{1}{2}$ lemon
1 sweet apple, peeled, cored
   and sliced

2 pears, peeled, cored and sliced
2 large oranges, peeled and
   segmented
1 small pineapple, peeled and cubed
2 tablespoons ($2\frac{1}{2}$T) orange
   flavoured liqueur

Dissolve the sugar with the water in a pan over low heat. Cool, then add the lemon juice. Pour into a rigid container. Mix in the prepared fruit.
To freeze: cover, label and freeze. When frozen transfer to a polythene bag, seal, label and return to freezer.
To thaw: thaw overnight in a refrigerator.
To serve: stir in liqueur before serving.
Serves 6

Lemon Cheesecake Pie–

Easy and Quick

Biscuit crust:
3 oz. (good cup) digestive biscuits (Graham crackers)

1½ oz. (3T) butter, melted
1 oz. (2T) castor (superfine) sugar

Filling:
8 oz. (1 cup) rich cream cheese
small (6 oz.) can (¾ cup) sweetened condensed milk

grated rind and juice of 2 large lemons
¼ pint (⅔ cup) double (heavy) cream

Crush the biscuits between 2 pieces of greaseproof paper with a rolling pin. Turn into a bowl and blend with the butter and sugar. Put the mixture in an 8 in. foil pie plate and press firmly into base, using back of a spoon.

Blend together all the filling ingredients. Spoon the mixture on to pie plate.

To freeze: cover loosely with foil and freeze until firm, then seal with a lid of foil, and put in a large polythene bag, label and return to freezer.

To thaw: remove polythene bag and foil and turn pie on to a serving plate. Decorate with whirls of cream and leave 1 hour at room temperature.

To serve: serve in slices.

Serves 6

Apricot Pie

Filling:
1 lb. (3 cups) dried apricots
3 oz. (⅜ cup) castor (superfine) sugar

½ oz. (⅛ cup) flaked almonds

Pastry:
12 oz. (3 cups) plain (all-purpose) flour
¼ teaspoon salt
4 oz. (8T) butter

3 oz. (6T) lard
about 12 teaspoons cold water
little icing (confectioners') sugar

Soak the apricots in cold water overnight. Next day, drain the apricots and put in pan. Cover with fresh cold water, add the sugar. Cover and simmer gently for about 1 hour or until tender. Cool before using.

Sift the flour and salt into a bowl. Rub in the fats until the mixture resembles breadcrumbs then add enough water to make a firm dough. Use half of the pastry to line a deep 9 in. foil plate. Add the apricots, and sprinkle the almonds on top. Top with the remaining pastry, sealing edges firmly.

To freeze: cover with foil, label and freeze.

To thaw: cook at 400°F, Mark 6 for about 45 minutes, or until pale golden-brown.

To serve: sprinkle with sieved icing (confectioners') sugar just before serving. Serve hot or cold with cream.

Variations: Use any fresh fruit for filling instead of dried apricots. Allow 4–6 oz. ($\frac{1}{2}$–$\frac{3}{4}$ cup) sugar for each pound of fruit. There is no need to cook the fruit first.

Serves 8

Bakewell Tart

Although this recipe does not contain ground almonds it is well worth making and is delicious for a family tea. Serve warm.

6 oz. shortcrust pastry made with
   6 oz. (1$\frac{1}{2}$ cups) flour etc. (see
   opposite)
Filling:

4 oz. (8T) butter	1 egg
4 oz. ($\frac{1}{2}$ cup) castor (superfine) sugar	$\frac{1}{2}$ teaspoon almond essence
4 oz. ($\frac{2}{3}$ cup) ground rice	1 heaped tablespoon (1$\frac{1}{4}$T) raspberry or strawberry jam

Use the pastry to line an 8 in. plain flan ring placed on a baking tray. Prick base with a fork, leave in a cold place 10 minutes.

Melt the butter for the filling in a pan. Stir in the sugar and cook for 1 minute. Add the ground rice, egg and essence. Cool slightly. Spread the jam in flan case. Pour in the filling.

Roll out the pastry trimmings and cut into $\frac{3}{4}$ in. wide strips. Arrange in lattice on top of the tart. Make them stick with a little milk. Cook at 400°F, Mark 6 for about 25 minutes, until well risen and golden brown. Remove from the tin and cool on a wire rack.

To freeze: pack in polythene bag, seal, label and freeze.

To thaw: thaw at room temperature for 6 hours then heat in the oven at 350°F, Mark 4 for 25 minutes.

To serve: serve warm.

Serves 6

Summer Pudding

*This really is the most unstodgy summer pudding that you could have.
It is my favourite pudding from the freezer and exceedingly good for a dinner
party if served with lashings of cream. This amount is for 4 puddings for 4
people. It is not worthwhile to make just one as the quantities of each fruit
would be so small. All the fruits used in the pudding could be ones from your
freezer. Vary the varieties if you like, but do include a fair amount of
strawberries as they have an excellent flavour.*

1 large white medium sliced loaf
  (about 20 slices) de-crusted
2 lb. prepared rhubarb
1 lb. redcurrants
$\frac{1}{2}$ lb. blackberries
1 lb. blackcurrants

$1-1\frac{3}{4}$ lb. ($2-3\frac{1}{2}$ cups) granulated
  sugar
$\frac{1}{4}$ pint ($\frac{2}{3}$ cup) water
2 lb. strawberries, sliced if large
$\frac{1}{2}$ lb. raspberries

Cut 6–8 slices of bread to fit the bases and tops of four 2 pint (5 cup)
pudding basins or straight-sided foil dishes. Cut the remaining bread
in fingers. Line the bases and sides of the basins with the bread. Put all the
fruit, except the strawberries and raspberries, and sugar to taste, in a pan
with the water. Cover and simmer gently until the fruit is almost soft,
then add the strawberries and raspberries and cook for a further 3
minutes. Put the mixture in the prepared basins, top with the remaining
slices of bread, pressing it down firmly. Cover each basin with a plate.
Press down with weights overnight.

To freeze: next day cover with foil, seal, label and freeze.

To thaw: thaw at room temperature for 8 hours or overnight in a
refrigerator.

To serve: turn out just before serving and decorate with whipped cream.
Serve with more cream.

Makes 4 puddings, each for 4 people

Profiteroles.

Summer Pudding.

Profiteroles

Choux Pastry:

4 oz. (1 cup) plain (all-purpose) flour

$\frac{1}{4}$ teaspoon salt

3 oz. (6T) butter or margarine

Filling and Sauce:

6 oz. (6 squares) plain chocolate

4 oz. ($\frac{1}{2}$ cup) castor (superfine) sugar

1 tablespoon ($1\frac{1}{4}$T) cocoa powder

$\frac{1}{2}$ pint ($1\frac{1}{4}$ cups), less 4 tablespoons (5T), water

4 eggs

$\frac{3}{4}$ pint (2 cups) water

2 eggs yolks

$\frac{1}{2}$ pint ($1\frac{1}{4}$ cups) double (heavy) cream, whipped

Sift together the flour and salt for pastry. Melt the butter with water in a pan and bring to the boil. Remove from the heat, add the flour all at once and beat in. Return to the heat and cook the flour, beating well until the paste is smooth and forms a ball in the pan. Cool slightly. Add the eggs, one at a time, beating well between each addition. Mixture should be smooth, glossy and of piping consistency. Place in a piping bag fitted with a $\frac{1}{2}$ in. plain nozzle. Pipe in small rounds, about size of a walnut, on greased and floured baking trays. Bake at 400°F, Mark 6 for 15–20 minutes until well risen. Make a hole in each bun to release the steam and return to the oven for a further 5 minutes to dry out. Cool on a wire rack.

Place the chocolate, sugar, cocoa and water in a pan and bring slowly to the bowl, stirring, until the chocolate has melted. Boil gently for 15 minutes. Remove from the heat and cool slightly. Beat in the egg yolks. Leave to cool. Fill profiteroles with cream. Pile up in a shallow dish and pour over the sauce. Hand round any remaining sauce separately.

To freeze:

Unbaked choux pastry: pipe on to a greased baking tray and open freeze (see page 47). When frozen remove from the tray and pack in polythene bags or heavy duty foil. Seal, label and return to freezer. Store up to 3 months.

To thaw: place the frozen shapes on a greased and floured baking tray and bake as above allowing 5 minutes longer.

Baked choux pastry: pack in polythene bags or foil and store in freezer up to 6 months.

To thaw: leave in packing at room temperature for about 1 hour, then remove the wrapping and refresh at 350°F, Mark 4 for 5 minutes, or place frozen in the oven and cook for 10 minutes. Cool before filling.

Strawberry Cheesecake

Crumb Crust:

4 oz. (1 good cup) digestive biscuits (Graham crackers), crushed

1 oz. (2T) demerara sugar

2 oz. (4T) butter, melted

Filling:

12 oz. (1½ cups) rich cream cheese

¼ pint (⅔ cup) single (light) cream

½ oz. (5 American teaspoons) powdered gelatine

4 tablespoons (5T) cold water

finely grated rind and juice of 2 large lemons

3 eggs, separated

4 oz. (½ cup) castor (superfine) sugar

¼ pint (⅔ cup) double (heavy) cream, lightly whipped

Decoration:

¼ lb. strawberries, halved and frozen

Lightly butter an 8 in. diameter, loose-bottomed cake tin or spring-form tin.

Blend together all the ingredients for the crumb crust and press into the base of the tin. Chill until firm.

Filling: blend together the cream cheese and thin cream. Dissolve the gelatine with the water in a bowl placed over a pan of simmering water. Place the lemon rind and juice, egg yolks and sugar in a bowl and whisk over a pan of simmering water until thick and foamy. Remove the bowl from the heat and continue to whisk the mixture until cool. Blend together the egg yolk mixture, gelatine and cream cheese mixture. When thick, but not set, fold in the whisked egg whites and thick cream, reserving 2 tablespoons (2½T) for decoration if liked. Turn the mixture into the cake tin.

To freeze: cover with foil and freeze until firm then remove from tin, wrap in foil, label and return to freezer.

To thaw: unwrap and place on a serving dish. Thaw in a refrigerator overnight or at room temperature for 8 hours.

To serve: decorate with cream, if used, and strawberries (see picture) 30 minutes before serving.

Serves 6

Crêpes Suzette

Batter:

4 oz. (1 cup) plain (all-purpose) flour

$\frac{1}{4}$ teaspoon salt

2 eggs

scant $\frac{1}{2}$ pint (1 cup) milk

1 tablespoon ($1\frac{1}{4}$ T) oil or melted butter

Sauce:

4 oz. ($\frac{1}{2}$ cup) castor (superfine) sugar

4 oz. (8T) butter

finely grated rind of 1 orange

juice of 2 oranges

1 tablespoon ($1\frac{1}{4}$ T) Grand Marnier or Curaçao

3 tablespoons ($3\frac{3}{4}$ T) brandy

oil for frying

Sift the flour and salt into a large bowl. Add the eggs, then gradually beat in half of the milk to make a smooth batter. Beat in the remaining milk. Finally stir in the oil or butter. Pour into a jug.

Pour a little oil into a 6 in. frying pan and heat until really hot. Pour off excess oil. Pour in enough batter, about 2 tablespoons ($2\frac{1}{2}$ T), to thinly coat the base of the pan, tilting the pan so that the base is evenly covered. Cook until the underside is golden brown, turn and cook the other side. Slip the pancake on to a wire cooling rack to cool. Repeat method, using the rest of the batter and oiling the pan between each pancake, to make 12 pancakes.

Sauce: place the sugar, butter, orange rind and juice in a large frying pan. Heat mixture gently until the sugar has dissolved, then simmer for 5–10 minutes until sauce is syrupy. Put a pancake into the sauce in the pan, and fold pancake in four. Remove the pancake from pan and place in rigid container. Repeat with remaining pancakes. When all the pancakes have been coated stir the liqueur and brandy into the sauce remaining in pan. Pour over the pancakes in the container.

To freeze: cover with a lid, label and freeze.

To thaw: place the frozen pancakes in a heavy, preferably non-stick, pan. Cover and re-heat at 350°F, Mark 4 for about 20 minutes, separating pancakes as they thaw.

To serve: serve hot.

Serves 4

Crêpes Suzettes.

Rum Chocolate Mousse

6 oz. (6 squares) plain chocolate,
  in small pieces
2 tablespoons (2½ T) water
3 tablespoons (3¾ T) rum
2 eggs, separated
¼ teaspoon vanilla essence
Decoration:
candied orange slices (see opposite) or

3 oz. (⅜ cup) castor (superfine)
  sugar
½ pint (1¼ cups) double (heavy)
  cream
¼ pint (⅔ cup) single (light)
  cream

chocolate curls (see below)

Line the base of an 8 in. cake tin or straight-sided soufflé dish with a
circle of non-stick silicone paper or greaseproof paper.
Melt the chocolate with the water and rum in a bowl placed over a pan
of hot water. Remove the bowl from the heat and blend in the egg
yolks and vanilla essence, then cool. In another bowl whisk the egg
whites until they form stiff peaks, then whisk in the sugar a teaspoon
at a time. Carefully fold the cooled chocolate mixture into the meringue.
Whisk the creams together until the mixture forms soft peaks, then fold
into chocolate mixture. Pour into the prepared tin or dish.
To freeze: freeze the mousse until firm then dip tin or dish in boiling
water for a few seconds. Turn out the mousse and put in a polythene
bag. Seal, label and return to freezer.
To thaw: turn the mousse onto a serving dish and thaw at room temperature
5–10 minutes.
To serve: decorate with halved candied orange slices or chocolate curls.
Serves 4

Chocolate Curls

Make chocolate curls by scraping chocolate from a slightly warmed block
of plain chocolate with a potato peeler. Keep in cool place until required.

Candied Orange Slices

1 thin-skinned orange

$3\frac{1}{2}$ oz. (scant $\frac{1}{2}$ cup) castor (superfine) sugar

Cut the orange in 12 thin slices. Halve each slice. Sprinkle the sugar on a large, flat plate and place the orange slices in a single layer on top. Leave at room temperature, turning two or three times, for 2 hours or until glazed. Remove from the plate and leave to dry slightly on greaseproof paper before use.

Straight from the Oven

Most baked items freeze particularly well, preserving the freshness which is such an important ingredient in the quality of cakes and bread. Yesterday's bread can become a thing of the past if you have a freezer in the house.

Walnut Bread

1 lb. (4 cups) plain (all-purpose) flour
4 teaspoons (2T) baking powder
8 oz. (1 cup) castor (superfine) sugar

4 oz. (1 cup) walnuts, chopped
12 oz. (1 cup) golden syrup
8 fl. oz. (1 cup) milk
2 eggs

Line two 2 lb. loaf tins (measuring 9 in. by 5 in. across the top) with greased greaseproof paper.
Sift the flour and baking powder into a bowl. Add the sugar and walnuts. Heat the syrup and milk gently in a pan until the syrup has melted. Pour on to the dry ingredients with the eggs and mix well. Divide the mixture between the prepared tins and bake at 325°F, Mark 3 for about 1 hour 15 minutes, or until centre of loaves spring back when lightly pressed with a finger. Turn out to cool on a wire rack.
To freeze: place in a polythene bag or wrap in foil when cold. Label and freeze.
To thaw: thaw overnight at room temperature, or for 2 hours in a warm room.
To serve: serve thinly sliced and buttered.
Makes 2 loaves.

Breads, Poppy Seed Twist, Cob, Fruit Loaf, Tea Ring and Rolls.

Basic White Bread

Use for loaves, rolls, pizza.

Yeast Liquid: 1 oz. fresh yeast (1 cake compressed yeast) blended with 1½ pints (scant 4 cups) milk or milk and water mixed

Or: dissolve 2 teaspoons sugar in 1½ pints (scant 4 cups) warm milk or milk and water mixed, sprinkle on 1 tablespoon (1¼T) dried yeast and leave until frothy, about 10 minutes.

Note: if risen dough is frozen before baking use 50% more yeast when making up dough for best results i.e. use 1½ oz. fresh yeast or 1½ level tablespoons (2T) dried yeast.

3 lb. (12 cups) plain flour
1 tablespoon (1¼T) salt

4 oz. (1½ cup) lard
or margarine

Prepare the yeast liquid. Mix the flour and salt and rub in the fat. Add the yeast liquid and work to a firm dough until the sides of the bowl are clean. Turn the dough on to a lightly floured surface and knead thoroughly until firm and elastic and no longer sticky. This will take about 10 minutes. To make in a mixing machine follow the manufacturers' instructions for the dough hook. Prepare the yeast liquid in the mixer bowl. Rub the fat into the flour and salt, add to the yeast liquid. Turn to the lowest speed and mix for 1–2 minutes to form dough. Increase the speed slightly and mix for further 2 minutes to knead dough.
Shape the dough into a ball and place in a large, lightly oiled polythene bag. Tie loosely at the top. Leave to rise until the dough doubles in size and springs back when pressed gently with a floured finger.

Rising times vary with temperatures:
Quick rise: About 1 hour in a warm place
Slower rise: 2 hours at average room temperature
Cold rise: 12–24 hours in a refrigerator.
              (Return to room temperature before shaping).

Turn the risen dough on to a lightly floured surface. Flatten with knuckles to knock out air bubbles and knead until the dough is firm, about 2 minutes.

To freeze risen dough: form into a cylindrical shape. Place in large, lightly oiled polythene bag. Seal tightly, label and keep in freezer up to 3 weeks.
To thaw: unseal polythene bag then tie loosely at top. Leave 5–6 hours at room temperature or overnight in refrigerator. Knock back if required, shape, prove and bake.

To freeze baked loaves and rolls: wrap in double thickness of foil or in polythene bags. If bread is likely to be required quickly always wrap in foil so that it can be placed frozen in a hot oven to thaw and refresh. Store 6–8 weeks.

To thaw: leave in packaging at room temperature. Loaves will take 3–4 hours, rolls 1–2 hours. Or leave overnight in refrigerator. Or place frozen, wrapped in foil, in a hot oven, 400°F, Mark 6. Loaves for 45 minutes, rolls for 15–20 minutes.

Rolls

Bridge Rolls: cut off and weigh 2 oz. pieces of risen dough, for each bridge roll. Use 3 oz. risen dough for larger rolls. Quickly knead each piece of dough and roll into a finger shape, about 4 inches long. Place on a greased baking tray.

Cottage Rolls: cut off and weigh 2 oz. pieces of risen dough for each roll. Cut a quarter off each 2 oz. piece of dough. Use largest piece to make a round roll. Place on a greased baking tray. Shape small piece into a small ball and place on top of larger roll. Push a floured finger through top roll until it touches baking tray. Brush with egg wash.

Knot Rolls: cut off and weigh 2 oz. pieces of risen dough for each roll. Roll each piece of dough into a 4–5 in. long strand. Tie in a loose knot. Place on a greased baking tray. Brush with egg wash and sprinkle with poppy seeds.

To rise: place baking tray inside a large, oiled polythene bag and leave to rise until dough doubles in size, about 30–40 minutes in a warm place. Bake at 400°F, Mark 6 for about 15–20 minutes.

Freeze: store and use as given in white dough recipe.

Cob

1 lb. 2 oz. risen dough

Shape dough into a round. Place in a greased, deep, 6 in. diameter cake tin. Place in a large, oiled polythene bag and leave to side until dough doubles in size, about 1 hour in a warm place. Bake 400°F, Mark 6 for about 35–40 minutes.

Cool, freeze and use as given in bread recipe.

Savarin

Yeast batter:

2 oz. ($\frac{1}{2}$ cup) plain flour

1 oz. fresh yeast (1 cake
   compressed yeast)

or

6 oz. ($1\frac{1}{2}$ cups) plain
   flour

$\frac{1}{2}$ teaspoon salt

1 oz. (2 tablespoons) castor sugar

1 level tablespoon
   dried yeast

6 tablespoons warm milk

4 eggs, beaten

4 oz. ($\frac{1}{2}$ cup) soft,
   not melted, butter

Rum syrup:

$1\frac{1}{4}$ lb. granulated sugar

1 pint ($2\frac{1}{2}$ cups) water

6–10 tablespoons rum

Glaze:

3 rounded tablespoons
   apricot jam

1 tablespoon water

Filling:

$\frac{1}{2}$ lb. strawberries, hulled

$\frac{1}{4}$ lb. green grapes

2–3 slices fresh pineapple,
   cut $\frac{1}{2}$ in. thick

In a large bowl mix together all yeast batter ingredients until smooth. Leave to stand until frothy, about 20 minutes for fresh yeast and 30 minutes for dried yeast. Add all remaining ingredients and beat thoroughly 3–4 minutes. Grease an 8–9 in. ring mould and half fill with dough. Place mould inside a large, oiled polythene bag and leave to rise almost to top of mould, about 30–40 minutes in a warm place. Bake in centre of oven, 400°F, Mark 6 for 20–25 minutes until deep golden brown. Leave to cool in tin for 5 minutes then turn out on to a wire rack and leave to cool.

To freeze: wrap in foil or put in a polythene bag, label and freeze up to 3 months.

To thaw: leave in packaging 2–3 hours at room temperature or overnight in refrigerator.

To serve: place thawed savarin in a fairly deep serving plate. Using a very fine skewer make holes all over top of savarin. Place sugar and water for syrup in heavy pan and dissolve sugar over low heat. Boil 1 minute, remove from heat and stir in rum. Spoon hot syrup over savarin. Pour any syrup which has drained into plate over savarin. Reserve about $\frac{1}{4}$ pint ($\frac{1}{2}$ cup) syrup. Warm apricot jam and water and sieve. Brush surface of savarin with glaze. If strawberries are large, cut in half. Halve and pip grapes. Cut pineapple in 1 in. pieces. Mix fruit with remaining syrup. Pile into centre of savarin. Serve with cream.

For 8–10

Savarin.

Poppy Seed Twist

12 oz. risen dough
egg wash made from 1 egg, 1
   teaspoon sugar and 1 tablespoon
   ($1\frac{1}{4}$T) water, beaten together

poppy seeds

Divide the dough in two equal pieces. Roll each to a 12–14 in. strand.
Pinch together one end of each strand and twist strands loosely. Pinch the
ends together. Tuck both ends under the twist and place on a greased
baking tray.
Brush with egg wash and sprinkle with poppy seeds. Place the tray in a
large, oiled polythene bag and leave to rise until dough doubles in size,
about 45–60 minutes in a warm place. Bake 400°F, Mark 6 for about
30 minutes.
Cool, freeze and use as given in bread recipe.

Fruit Loaf

1 lb. risen dough
2 oz. ($\frac{1}{3}$ cup) sultanas
   (seedless white raisins)

1 oz. ($\frac{1}{6}$ cup) chopped
   peel
grated rind of 1 lemon

Work together all the ingredients. Press the dough into an oblong same
width as a 1 lb. loaf tin. Fold in three and turn over so the seam is
underneath. Smooth over the top, tuck in ends and place in greased tin.
Place the tin in a large, oiled polythene bag and leave to rise until dough
doubles in size or rises to top of tin, about 1 hour in a warm place. Bake at
400°F, Mark 6 for about 30–35 minutes.
Cool, freeze and use as given in bread recipe.

Iced Tea Ring

12 oz. risen dough
Filling:
$\frac{1}{2}$ oz. (1T) butter, melted
2 oz. ($\frac{1}{4}$ cup) soft brown
    sugar
Icing:
2 oz. ($\frac{1}{2}$ cup) icing (confectioners)
    sugar, sieved
1 teaspoon warm water

1 teaspoon cinnamon
1 oz. ($\frac{1}{4}$ cup) almonds, finely
    chopped

$\frac{1}{2}$ oz. ($\frac{1}{8}$ cup) flaked almonds,
    toasted
glacé (candied) cherries

Roll out the dough to a 12×9 in. rectangle. Brush with melted butter and sprinkle with brown sugar, cinnamon and chopped almonds. Roll up firmly and seal edges. Bring the roll ends together to form a ring, seal ends and place on a greased baking tray. With scissors make cuts, 1 in. apart and to within $\frac{1}{2}$ in. of centre. Separate by turning each piece carefully sideways.

Place inside a large, oiled polythene bag and leave to rise until dough doubles in size, about 45–60 minutes in a warm place. Bake at 400°F, Mark 6 for 30 minutes. Cool then mix together icing sugar and water and trickle over ring. Decorate the top with almonds and halved cherries.

Note: the Tea Ring can be frozen iced but cannot then be refreshed in a hot oven before serving.

Scottish Shortbread

Shortbread will keep well for a couple of weeks in an air-tight tin but it will keep much longer if stored in your freezer. When it thaws it is full of flavour and beautifully crisp.

4 oz. (1 cup) plain (all-purpose) flour
2 oz. ($\frac{1}{3}$ cup) cornflour (cornstarch)

4 oz. (8T) butter
2 oz. ($\frac{1}{4}$ cup) castor (superfine) sugar
little extra castor (superfine) sugar

Sift together the flour and cornflour. In another bowl cream the butter until soft then beat in the castor (superfine) sugar. Blend in the sifted flours a tablespoon at a time. Knead mixture together, place on 7 × 11 in. swiss roll tin and roll out or press out with flat of the hand. Prick well with a fork. Sprinkle with castor (superfine) sugar. Chill in a refrigerator for 15 minutes then bake at 325°F, Mark 3 for 35 minutes or until pale golden-brown. Cool on a baking tray for a few minutes then transfer to a wire rack to finish cooling.
To freeze: wrap in foil, label and freeze.
To thaw: thaw at room temperature for 2–3 hours.
Makes 8 pieces

Scottish Shortbread.

Small Mince Pies

8 oz. rich shortcrust pastry
    made with 8 oz. (2 cups) flour,
    etc. or
    13 oz. packet (package) frozen
    pastry, thawed
Filling:
1 lb. jar mincemeat
Glaze:
milk   icing (confectioners') sugar

Make the pastry in the usual way and chill before using. Roll out the pastry thinly on floured table, then cut 12 rounds with a 3 in. fluted cutter, and 12 with a $2\frac{3}{4}$ in. cutter. Place 12 larger rounds in greased patty tins and put a heaped teaspoon of mincemeat in centre of each. Moisten edges with water and place a second pastry circle on each. Prick tops and glaze with milk. Bake at 425°F, Mark 7 for about 20 minutes. Cool on a wire rack.

To freeze: put mince pies in a polythene bag and seal or wrap in foil. Label and freeze.

To thaw: place frozen pies on a baking tray and re-heat at 425°F, Mark 7 for about 15 minutes.

To serve: serve warm, dusted with icing (confectioners') sugar.

Makes 12

Scones

8 oz. (2 cups) self-raising
    flour
pinch of salt
2 oz. (4T) butter

2 oz. ($\frac{1}{4}$ cup) castor (superfine)
    sugar
$\frac{1}{4}$ pint ($\frac{2}{3}$ cup) milk
little extra milk

Sift the flour and salt into a bowl. Rub in the butter until mixture resembles breadcrumbs. Add the sugar and sufficient milk to make a firm dough. Roll out on to a lightly floured board, then cut in rounds with a $1\frac{1}{2}$ in. plain cutter. Place on a greased baking tray and brush with remaining milk. Bake at 425°F, Mark 7 for 10–15 minutes, until well risen and golden brown. Cool on a wire rack.

To freeze: put in polythene bags, seal, label and freeze.
To thaw: re-heat at 350°F, Mark 4 for about 15 minutes.
To serve: serve split and buttered.
Variations:
Fruit scones: add 2 oz. currants or sultanas ($\frac{1}{3}$ cup) to basic mixture.
Cheese scones: omit the sugar. Add 3 oz. ($\frac{3}{4}$ cup) finely grated Cheddar cheese and use a mixture of equal parts milk and water instead of all milk.
Makes about 15

Farmhouse Fruit Cake

10 oz. ($2\frac{1}{2}$ cups) self-raising flour
$\frac{1}{4}$ teaspoon salt
8 oz. (1 cup) butter
8 oz. (1 cup) castor (superfine) or soft brown sugar
grated rind of 1 orange
5 eggs

1 lb. (3 cups) currants and sultanas (seedless white raisins), mixed
4 oz. ($\frac{2}{3}$ cup) candied peel, chopped
4 oz. ($\frac{1}{2}$ cup) glacé (candied) cherries, quartered
1 tablespoon ($1\frac{1}{4}$T) golden syrup

Line an 8 in. diameter cake tin with greaseproof paper, then grease.
Sift together the flour and salt. Cream the butter until soft. Add the sugar and orange rind and beat until light and fluffy. Add the eggs, gradually, beating well after each addition. Fold in the flour and fruits. Stir in the syrup.
Turn into prepared tin. Bake at 300°F, Mark 2 for $2\frac{1}{2}$ hours, or until a skewer inserted in the centre of the cake comes out clean. Cool in the tin for 10 minutes, then turn out on to a wire rack and leave until cold.
To freeze: wrap in a double thickness of foil, label and freeze.
To thaw: loosen the foil slightly and leave at room temperature for 6 hours, or overnight.

Coffee Gâteau

3 large eggs
3 oz. ($\frac{3}{8}$ cup) castor
  (superfine) sugar
Butter Icing:
12 oz. ($2\frac{1}{4}$ cups) icing
  (confectioners') sugar,
  sieved
2 tablespoons ($2\frac{1}{2}$ T) coffee
  essence or strong coffee
2 tablespoons ($2\frac{1}{2}$ T) rum or brandy

3 oz. ($\frac{3}{4}$ cup) self-raising flour,
  sieved

6 oz. ($\frac{3}{4}$ cup) butter
1 oz. ($\frac{1}{4}$ cup) crystallised ginger
2 oz. ($\frac{1}{2}$ cup) blanched almonds,
  chopped or flaked then
  lightly toasted
few chocolate balls or chocolate
  nuts

Grease two $7\frac{1}{2}$ in. diameter straight-sided sandwich tins, then line the bases with a circle of greased, greaseproof paper.

Whisk the eggs and sugar in a bowl placed over a pan of hot water until the mixture is pale and mousse-like. Remove the bowl from the heat and fold in the flour, using a metal spoon. Divide the mixture between the prepared tins and bake at 375°F, Mark 5 for 20–25 minutes, or until the centre of each sponge springs back when lightly pressed. Turn out and cool on a wire rack.

Blend together the icing sugar, coffee and rum or brandy for butter icing. Cream the butter until soft, add the icing sugar mixture a little at a time, beating well after each addition.

Put just under half of the butter icing in a bowl. Chop the ginger and add to this mixture. Cut the sponges in half and sandwich together with some of the mixture. Use the remainder to sandwich two sponges together. Put one heaped tablespoon ($1\frac{1}{4}$ T) of butter icing aside in a small bowl. Spread the remaining butter icing round the sides and over the top of the cake. Press half of the almonds against sides of cake with a palette knife. Decorate the top with remaining almonds. Pipe with the remainder of cream in rosettes (see picture).

To freeze: open freeze (see page 47) then place in a polythene bag, seal, label and freeze.

To thaw: remove from the bag, place on a serving plate and thaw at room temperature for 5 hours. Decorate with chocolate balls.

To serve: serve in slices.

Makes 8–10 slices

Coffee Gâteau.

A birthday cake with the names of all the guests at the party.

Birthday Cake

This cake can be made well ahead and put in the freezer, all but for putting the candles on and the ribbon round the outside. The icing is lemon icing which freezes well. Royal icing cracks on thawing so is not advisable. If you prefer, make just the sponge cake base and freeze that. Then ice it the day before the birthday.

Victoria Sponge Base:

8 oz. (1 cup) butter

8 oz. (1 cup)
caster sugar

finely grated rind
of 2 lemons

4 large eggs, beaten

8 oz. (2 cups) self-raising
flour

about 2 tablespoons
milk

Lemon Butter Icing:

4 oz. ($\frac{1}{2}$ cup) butter

8 oz. (2 cups) icing

(confectioners) sugar

juice of $\frac{1}{2}$ lemon

Almond Paste for Top of Cake:

4 oz. (1 cup) ground almonds

2 oz. ($\frac{1}{2}$ cup) icing
(confectioners) sugar, sieved

3 tablespoons apricot jam

2 oz. ($\frac{1}{4}$ cup)
caster sugar

1 egg white

1 tablespoon water

Lemon glace icing:

12 oz. (3 cups) icing
(confectioners) sugar, sieved

about 4 tablespoons lemon juice

$\frac{1}{2}$ oz. (1 tablespoon)
butter

pink colouring

Line a deep 10 in. cake tin with greased greaseproof paper. Beat together butter, sugar and lemon rind for cake base until light and fluffy. Gradually beat in eggs. Fold in flour with sufficient milk to make a soft dropping consistency. Turn into prepared tin and bake 350°F, Mark 4 about 50 minutes or until centre of cake springs back when lightly pressed with a finger. Turn out to cool on a wire rack. Beat together all ingredients for lemon butter icing. Split cake in half and sandwich together again with icing. Blend together ground almonds, sugars and egg white for almond paste then knead by hand to form a smooth paste. Heat jam and water together in a small pan then sieve. Use glaze to brush top and sides of cake. Roll out almond paste to a 10 in. circle, using cake tin as a guide. Place almond paste on top and press down firmly. Heat together sugar, lemon juice and butter in a pan over very low heat, mixing well. Take out 2 tablespoons icing and put on one side. Add few drops pink colouring to icing remaining in pan. Thin down slightly with a little water. Place cake on a thin, 10 in. silver board. Pour over pink icing so that top is completely coated. Put on one side to dry for several hours or overnight. Put remaining white icing in a piping bag fitted with a plain writing nozzle. Divide the cake in sections with icing and write a name in each section as shown in picture.

To freeze: open freeze (see page 47) then wrap in foil, label and return to freezer.

To thaw: remove foil and thaw cake at room temperature for 8 hours.

To serve: decorate with $1\frac{1}{4}$ yards striped ribbon and $1\frac{1}{4}$ yards deeper pink see-through ribbon (see picture). Finish with bows made from left-over ribbon and place a candle on each section of cake.

Variations:

Orange Victoria Sandwich

Use half the amount of ingredients and substitute the grated rind of one orange and one tablespoon ($1\frac{1}{4}$T) orange juice for the lemon rind and milk. Divide the mixture between two greased 7 in. diameter sandwich tins and bake at 350°F, Mark 4 for about 20 minutes.

For the butter icing:

3 oz. (6T) butter

6 oz. ($1\frac{1}{4}$ cups) icing (confectioners') sugar, sieved

grated rind and juice of 1 small orange

Cream together these ingredients and use to sandwich the sponges together.

To freeze: wrap in foil, label and freeze.

To thaw: thaw for 3–4 hours at room temperature.

To serve: dust the top with castor (superfine) sugar.

Chocolate Victoria Sandwich:

Make as above, omitting the orange from sponge and icing, and adding $\frac{1}{2}$ oz. ($\frac{1}{4}$ cup) cocoa and 1 oz. (1 square) plain melted chocolate to the sponge. Use 5 oz. ($1\frac{1}{4}$ cups) icing (confectioners') sugar and $\frac{1}{2}$ oz. ($\frac{1}{8}$ cup) cocoa for the butter icing.

Butter Crunch Biscuits

8 oz. (2 cups) plain (all-purpose) flour
pinch of salt
6 oz. ($\frac{3}{4}$ cup) butter
finely grated rind of $\frac{1}{2}$ lemon

4 oz. ($\frac{1}{2}$ cup) castor (superfine) sugar
1 oz. (2 tablespoons) granulated sugar

Sift the flour and salt into a bowl. Cream the butter until soft, add lemon rind and castor (superfine) sugar and beat until light and fluffy. Blend in the flour and mix until smooth.

Divide into two equal portions. Roll both out on a board coated with granulated sugar to form two 6 in. long sausage shapes. Wrap in foil and chill in a refrigerator until firm.

To freeze: cut each roll into about 16 slices. Place on a baking tray and open freeze (see page 47). Pack in rigid boxes, cover, label and freeze.

To thaw: place biscuits on baking trays, leaving each room to spread. Bake at 325°F, Mark 3 for 40 minutes or until pale golden round edges.

To serve: cool on a wire rack and store in an airtight tin until required.

Makes about 32

Lemon Curd

Lemon curd normally does not keep well and should be eaten within six weeks. With a freezer you can keep it for six months.

4 oz. (8T) butter
8 oz. (1 cup) castor (superfine) sugar

2 large lemons
2 large eggs

Put the butter and sugar in the top part of a double saucepan with boiling water in lower part. Stir well until butter has melted. (If you do not have a double saucepan use a basin over a pan of water.) Blend the finely grated lemon rind with eggs in a bowl. Squeeze juice from the lemons and strain on to eggs. Add the mixture to the butter and sugar in the pan and cook over hot, but not boiling, water. Stir constantly until the mixture is thick enough to coat back of a wooden spoon. Pour into small foil containers.

To freeze: cool, then cover with a lid of foil, label and freeze.

To thaw: thaw at room temperature for 2–3 hours or in a refrigerator overnight.

Index

All recipes indicate how to freeze, thaw and serve. Figures in italics refer to illustrations.

Alarm systems for freezers 13
Aluminium foil, for freezer packaging 20, 21–4, *22*
Apples, freezing of raw 32, 44
Apricot pie 100–1
Artichoke soup 50
Ascorbic acid, used in freezing fruit 44, *47*
Austrian rum dessert cake 97

Baby foods, freezing of 29–30, *31*
Bacon and onion quiche 66, *67*
Bacon, freezing of 25, 34
Bakewell tart 101
Beefburgers, freezing of 32
Beef goulash 72–3
Beef Kromeskies 73
Beef Stroganoff 69
Birthday cake *123*, 124–5
Blanching baskets 24, *26*, *27*
Blanquette de veau 78, *79*
Boeuf Bourguignonne 68–9
Bread
    basic white 112
    freezing of 32
    walnut 110
Breadcrumbs, freezing of 30
Bulk buying 24–5
Butter crunch biscuits 126
Butter, freezing of 29

Cakes
    birthday *123*, 124–5
    coffee Gâteau 122, *123*
    farmhouse fruit 121
    lemon cheesecake pie 100
    strawberry cheesecake *11*, 105
Candied orange slices 109
Canelloni on savoury spinach 60
Cauliflower au gratin 90
Cheese, freezing of 29
Cheese, freezing of grated 30
Cheese sauce 60
Chest freezer 9
    packing food in a 20
Chicken
    cidered 84
    country pie 81
    mild curried 82, *83*
    ,stock 91
Chicken carcasses for stock, freezing of 30
Chocolate Victoria sandwich cake 125
Chops, freezing of 34, *39*
Choux pastry 104
Cidered chicken 84
Cob *111*, 113
Coffee gâteau 122, *123*
Colour identification used for packing food 20, 21, *23*
Conservators 12
Containers
    choice of 17–20

polythene rigid *19*, 21–3
Cooking fat, storage time for 29
Cooking methods for frozen vegetables 37–42
Cream, freezing of 29
Crêpes Suzette 106, *107*
Croûtons, freezing of 30
Curried shepherd's pie 76–7
Cutlets, freezing of 34, *39*

Dairy produce, method of freezing 29–30
Deep freezing, defined 33
    maximum amount of food at one time 32
Defrosting of freezer 14
Desserts
    apricot pie 100–1
    Austrian rum dessert cake 97
    bakewell tart 101
    candied orange slices 109
    Crêpe Suzette 106, *107*
    fresh fruit salad 98
    ice cream 92–3
    iced lemon soufflés 96
    iced lemon syllabub cream 96–7
    iced strawberry soufflés 93
    lemon cheesecake pie 100
    oranges in liqueur 98, *99*
    orange sorbet 94
    pineapple ice cream 94, *95*
    Profiteroles 104
    rum chocolate mousse 108
    strawberry cheesecake *11*, 105
    summer pudding 102, *103*
Dog meat, freezing of 34

Eggs, method of freezing 29, 30

Fish fingers, freezing of 32
Fish, method of freezing 29
Foil
    bags 24
    dishes and plates for freezer packaging 24
    see also Aluminium foil
Foods, general hints on how to freeze 28–49
Freezer
    advice on prices 12
    alarm system for 13
    basic foods to store in 16–17
    choice of position of 13
    colour identification and charts used for food in 20, *23*
    containers used for freezing food 20
    defrosting of 14
    equipment for freezer 24
    foods not suitable for storage in 17
    general maintenance for 14
    guide lines to purchase a 9–13
    how to use a 16–27
    importance of internal light in 13
    insuring food contents of 13
    internal maintenance of 14
    locks for 12
    packing food for 17–20, 28

packing materials 21–4
packing of food in 20–4, 28
possible failures of 13
preparing a new 14
protection of exterior 14
quick-freezing compartment in 12
required size of 9–12
second-hand 12
servicing of 14
setting of temperature gauge on 14
taping of freezer plug 13, *15*
types of 9–13
usual extras for 12
Freezer burn, defined 32
Freezer record book *18*, 20–1
Freezer/refrigerator, combined 9, *10*
Freezer tape 24
Frikadeller with onion sauce 76
Fruit
    freezing of 42–9, *46*
    grey deposit on 32
    layering with sugar 44, *47*
    open freezing of *47*
    packing of frozen 44–9
    preparation for freezing 44–9
    special tips for freezing 44–9
    syrup strengths for frozen 42, *47*
    thawing of 44
Fruit loaf *111*, 116
Fruit salad, fresh 98

Glass jars for use in freezer 24
Grouse, casseroled 89

Haddock fish cakes, smoked 64
Hare, jugged 88–9
Headspace, defined 33
Heat-sealing equipment 24
Herbs, freezing of *35*, 37
Hot-cross buns, freezing of 30

Ice cream 92–3
    freezing of 32
Ice cubes
    flavoured 30, *35*
    storing of in freezer 30
Insurance for contents of freezer 13
Internal light in freezers, importance of 12

Kidneys, sherried 86–7

Labels used for foods in freezer 24, 28, 34, 37
Lamb goulash, paprika 85
Lamb in barbecue sauce, foiled 84
Lancashire hot pot 86
    Lasagne al Forno 74, *75*
Lemon cheesecake pie 100
Lemon curd 126
Lemon soufflés, iced 96
Lemon Syllabub cream, iced 96–7
Liver and onions, braised 88
Lock on freezer 12

Mackerel pâté, smoked 54, *55*
Meat
    method of freezing 33–6, *39*

preparation to freeze 34
roasting, boiling and stewing
    frozen 36
storage times 34
thawing and cooking 34–6
Melon balls, chilled 58
Melon cocktail 59
Milk, freezing of 29, 32
Mince pies, small 120
Minced meat, freezing of 34
Moussaka 87
Mustard dip, American 59

Nutritional values in frozen foods 8

Offal, freezing of 34
Onions, freezing of prepared 30
Onion soup, French 53
Oranges in liqueur 98, 99
Orange sorbet 94
Oranges (whole Seville), freezing of 30
Orange Victoria sandwich cake 125
Osso Buco 11, 80

Packing food for the freezer 17–24, 28
Packing
    materials 21–4, 28
    of fruit 44
    of vegetables 37–42
Paper (moisture and vapour-proof)
    for freezer packaging 24
Paprika lamb goulash 85
Pâté
    farmhouse 57
    quick 58
    smoked mackerel 54, 55
Pineapple ice cream 94, 95
Pizza 62, 63
Plug for freezer, taping of 13, 15
Polythene bags and sheeting for

freezer packaging 21, 24, 28
Poppy seed twist 111, 116
Pork, creamed 77
Potato and leek soup 51, 52
Potatoes, chipped, freezing of 32
Potatoes, piped duchess 90
Poultry and game, freezing of 34
Profiteroles 104

Quiche, bacon and onion 66, 67
Quick freezing compartment 12

Ratatouille 60
Re-freezing of foods 32
Rice, to freeze long grain 91
Rolls 111
    bridge 113
    cottage 113
    knot 113
Rum chocolate mousse 108

Sandwiches, freezing of 30
Sausage rolls 68
    freezing of 30
Sausages, freezing of 34
Savarin 114, 115
Saw or serrated knives for cutting
    frozen food 24
Scallops mornay 11, 56
Scones 120–1
    freezing of 30
Scottish shortbread 118, 119
Shepherd's pie, curried 76–7
Small mince pies 120
Sole à la Bonne Femme 65
Soup
Artichoke 50
French onion soup 53
potato and leek 51, 52
taramasalata 52

Spinach, canelloni on savoury 60
Steak and kidney pies 70, 71
Steak, kidney and mushroom pie,
    large 72
Steaks, freezing of 34, 39
Storage time
    cooked dishes 33
    exceeding 33
    fruit 44–9
    meats 34
    vegetables 37–42
Strawberry cheese cake 11, 105
Strawberry soufflés, iced 93
Summer pudding 102
Syrup strengths for frozen fruits 42

Taramasalata 52
Tea ring 111
    iced 117
Thawing methods 28
    for fruits 44
    for vegetables 37–42
Thermometer for freezer 24
Twists for packaging in freezer 24

Upright freezer 9
    packing food into an 20

Vegetables, blanching of before
    freezing 33, 37, 43
    cooking and draining before
        freezing 37
    freezing of 32, 37–42
    packing and labelling 37–42
    preparation methods for freezing
        37–42
    special tips for freezing 37–42
    thawing and cooking of 37–42

Walnut bread 110
Weights and measures 6